D0322025

The Performance Coaching Toolkit

The
Performance
Coaching
Toolkit

Angus McLeod and Will Thomas

Open University Press

Open University Press
McGraw-Hill Education
McGraw-Hill House
Shoppenhangers Road
Maidenhead
Berkshire
England
SL6 2QL

email: enquiries@openup.co.uk
world wide web: www.openup.co.uk

and Two Penn Plaza, New York, NY 10121-2289, USA

First published 2010

Copyright © Will Thomas and Angus McLeod 2010

All rights reserved. Except for the quotation of short passages for the purposes of criticism and review, no part of this publication may be reproduced, stored in a retrieval system, or transmitted, in any form or by any means, electronic, mechanical, photocopying, recording or otherwise, without the prior written permission of the publisher or a licence from the Copyright Licensing Agency Limited. Details of such licences (for reprographic reproduction) may be obtained from the Copyright Licensing Agency Ltd of Saffron House, 6–10 Kirby Street, London, EC1N 8TS.

A catalogue record of this book is available from the British Library

ISBN-13: 978-0-33-523890-3 (pb)
ISBN-10: 0335238904 (pb)

Library of Congress Cataloging-in-Publication Data
CIP data applied for

Typeset by RefineCatch Limited, Bungay, Suffolk
Printed and bound in the UK by Bell and Bain Ltd, Glasgow

Fictitious names of companies, products, people, characters and/or data that may be used herein (in case studies or in examples) are not intended to represent any real individual, company, product or event.

Mixed Sources
Product group from well-managed forests and other controlled sources
www.fsc.org Cert no. TT-COC-002769
© 1996 Forest Stewardship Council
FSC

The *McGraw·Hill* Companies

Contents

About the Authors

Angus McLeod is well known internationally as a coach. He has published a number of books and about thirty papers in international journals on coaching and leadership as well as numerous web-based articles. He designed the enormously successful performance coaching courses offered by Newcastle College creating many thousands of diploma graduates at both standard and advanced levels. His master-classes in coaching have been attended and filmed around the world. His work has been the subject of several separate modelling projects to define how he produces extraordinary results from a facilitation process based upon coaching. He co-founded the Coaching Foundation, a not-for-profit group offering development opportunities to a wide range of coaches at all levels. He coaches internationally and his business, Angus McLeod Associates, provides coaches and coach-training across a phenomenal range of sectors from manufacturing industry to government, finance and healthcare. Much of his training work is on bringing coaching skills into the working style of managements. As he says, 'You actually do not need to know very much about a sector to make an impact with either coaching or culture-change if you use a proven coaching model.'

Among Angus's other publications are:

Performance Coaching
Me, Myself, My Team
Self Coaching Leadership

Will Thomas is an award-winning author, coach and trainer. He wrote *Coaching Solutions*, the first book of its kind to bring coaching into the world of education and he has gone on to write eight other books, including three toolkits in the fields of coaching, creativity and leadership. His work in schools, colleges and universities is well known. He is a renowned consultant to organizations, developing wider coaching models in local authorities, schools and colleges in the UK and abroad. He has trained over 15,000 teachers and leaders in coaching techniques, and founded the Institute of Education Coaching in 2006 to oversee the development of high quality and accredited education coaching. A passionate advocate of opportunity for all, Will is principal advisor to the Manisha Child Welfare Foundation, Nepal, and supports the development of some of the remotest schools in the world.

Among Will's other publications are:

Coaching Solutions
Coaching Solutions Resource Book
Creative Teaching and Learning Toolkit
Creative Teaching and Learning Resource Book
Everything You Need to Know about Teaching, But Are Too Busy to Ask

Foreword

In *Performance Coaching Toolkit*, Will and Angus have provided a rich mixture of techniques from a wide range of sources and, importantly, from their own wide experience. The techniques are spelled out clearly with triggers, rationale, instructions for use, and links to other tools, making this a very clear, useable manual. More than a manual the book explores the place of tools in our development as coaches. It emphasizes philosophy and dynamics above mere technique – humanity and principles are more important than skills.

This book is full of learned wisdom and wise sayings – I particularly liked 'Let silence do the heavy lifting'. The chapter on clean language I found particularly useful for my own practice and I also valued the chapter at the end which compares the book's central STEPPPA model with GROW and STRIDE as alternative frameworks for a coaching or a mentoring session. The scaled coaching skills checklist, from emergent to establishing to excelling, is also a useful tool for developing coaches.

David Megginson
Emeritus Professor of HRD
Coaching and Mentoring Research Unit
Sheffield Hallam University

Acknowledgements

I acknowledge that there are forces overt and hidden in one's learning and I am grateful for both. I remain aware that learning grows and that setting down new thoughts with an open heart stimulates more creativity. In this process, the sheer genius of Will Thomas is notable – the word co-creation could quite easily be branded to him and I look forward to our joint progress and sharing that progress with you.

Angus McLeod

I wish to thank everyone whom I have coached over the past 15 years. Their responses and feedback have been enormously helpful in shaping the coach I am today. Particular thanks go to my family for their support in the ups and downs of running a business, writing books and generally living in challenging times. Love to Richard, Mum, Dad, and Sal. I would like to dedicate this book to my Dad for his 70th birthday in 2010.

It remains a great pleasure and privilege to work alongside Angus, the ease of working and sheer creative energy and humour that he brings to our writing partnership are immensely rewarding.

Will Thomas

List of Tools

Introduction

Coaching, as we identify it, has to achieve the **coachee**'s **outcomes**. It will invariably increase both their performance and their well-being. Performance on its own can be achieved without coaching over short periods, especially if the need for performance is obvious. In contrast, for an individual to have sustainable performance, they need to develop well-being (as well as performance). The addition of well-being maintains both confidence and motivation and lowers the risk of burn-out. Pushing people too hard may sometimes make them more efficient in that moment but produces lower overall efficacy in the mid to long term.

Coaching provides a key philosophy for developing both well-being and performance in people. Underpinning that philosophy are key skills. *The Performance Coaching Toolkit* is concentrated unashamedly on key skills and **tool**s – yet underpinning these is a strong set of principles which cannot be divorced from the use of tools and techniques. Who you are as a **coach**, in other words, who you are 'being' when you are with your coachees, is central to that relationship. If coachees and their **client** organizations are going to significantly benefit from the process, the qualities of being are more critical to performance than the tools selected.

This book is an evolution from *Performance Coaching: The Handbook for Managers, HR Professionals and Coaches* by McLeod (2003a). *The Performance Coaching Toolkit* enhances, in very practical terms, the body of work contained in that widely recognized book. It is also enriched by methods taken from our joint understanding and development of practical learning technology and from our work in education, personal development and in organizations. This book can be used entirely as a stand-alone toolkit for coaching 'best practice' whether in formal coaching spaces or informal settings. It is also designed to support 'conversational coaching' – a process of coaching that is used fluidly, episode by episode, throughout the day.

The approach used here is concise and immediately helpful – you will know how and when to use specific coaching tools to best effect. We believe that this Toolkit is suited to coaches and prospective coaches in all sectors, particularly those who want rapid accessibility to understanding coaching practice. It is also suited to those simply wanting a reliable source book for coaching methods. We have very deliberately included linguistic **triggers** in this text to help coaches use the right set of tools in their actual coaching sessions, without having to pause in their work.

For further learning integration and to make some of the tools more comprehensible in real life, we offer a few stories which illustrate both the theoretical approach and sometimes also show natural divergence from the tools that occur in real-life management.

We present an easily understandable structure for coaching so that all the tools sit simply within a practical framework for developing and enhancing your own coaching style. This framework, the **STEPPPA** Model, also provides a coherent and practical model for keeping in touch with the coaching process as a structured journey.

You will quickly recognize a layout that becomes familiar and promotes very fast access to key information. Links between other related models and tools are provided throughout, so the complexity of the coaching process, with time, becomes even more comprehensible.

In your journey to enhancing the performance and well-being of the people around you, we trust that this book will serve you well.

Learning from this book

We've put a lot of thought into the writing and design of the book. We want it to be the most user-friendly coaching book you've ever read and so we have included several innovations and features to make this possible. They include:

- navigational devices to help you find your way through the book;

- diagrams, tables and other images to enhance the visual appeal of the text.

- the availability of the tools online for you to download. To download tools amd more visit: www.performancecoachingtoolkit.com

There is also productive emphasis, via exercises, on practical strategies and self-reflection (on your own coaching skills).

There are 51 tools in the Toolkit, aimed at individuals, managers, and HR professionals in all settings. The book is made interactive through the use of a 'coaching skills checklist' which can help provide a structured path for improving your coaching. The world of the coachee's **experience** will become more familiar to you and this will further help to advise you in the use of the tools. If you're serious about making positive changes, then we strongly recommend that you use the framework to plan and review your progress; this will help you to create a powerful personal action plan. We also encourage you to carry out the exercises we've included in Part 3, to enable you to develop your core coaching skills.

The text in the tools is directed at coaches and managers but, in contrast, the exercises are couched for *anyone* doing those exercises – we would urge coaches to be familiar with any exercise before offering it to their coachees – to do that, the coach/manager needs to fully complete them also.

Words in <this type of parenthesis> indicate an instruction to the coach during an example question or dialogue.

We have used the terms '**target**' and 'goal' interchangeably with emphasis on 'target' as this is part of the **acronym** for a coaching structure used throughout the Toolkit. Outcomes are not always the same as targets and can be in conflict. This distinction is made and clarified in the text.

We've also included an extensive glossary of terms used in the book, allowing you to quickly check any terminology you're not familiar with. The first use of any word in the glossary is emboldened in the text.

Angus McLeod and Will Thomas
September 2009

PART

Orientation

CHAPTER 1

Key Issues in Coaching

Coaching is a **facilitation** process in which the coach, most often, does not instruct or direct the coachee. Coaching is not a solution for all the people all of the time, but it does create in all coachees, the most motivated, successful and developmental outcomes one can possibly hope to see when developing other people.

- Coaching does not sustain coachee-dependence, it creates independence.

- Coaching does not crush independent thinking and creativity as the one-up approaches of telling and directing do.

- Coaching creates coachee-solutions but also enhances the ability of the coachee to self-**challenge** and to apply their learning in other situations and in other **contexts**.

In the next chapter we will enhance understanding about when and where to use coaching instead of other types of managing methodologies, including **mentoring** and directing.

To be a coach and/or 'coaching manager' one needs to be flexible in approach and that **flexibility** will be driven by the needs of the individual(s).

The coach/manager puts judgements and plans aside – evidence on which decisions are made is obtained from the individual/coachee. Ideally, if the individual/coachee is competent, they set their own targets and plans, with or without the help of their coach/manager.

Richard Greenleaf (Greenleaf and Spears 1998) coined the term '**Servant Leadership**'. Servant leadership is a useful place to start in setting up one's psyche for coaching and managing. It means that the leader is also the servant to those who work for them. The coach/leader nurtures, helps the coachee to explore their thinking, to get in touch with both their energies and their fears and to be successful, on a repeated and growing basis.

In this book, detailing as it does the powerful tools of our trade, it may seem odd to quote Tim Gallwey (1999), the so-called 'grandfather' of modern coaching, who said, 'Principles are more important than tools.' Principles do frame the use of the tools and without a psychologically-healthy approach to coaching, predicated upon sound principles, the tools will only be applied ineptly. We prefer the epithet, 'humanity and principles are more important than skills'. These together set the psychological and emotional framework for the most exquisite leading and coaching.

The McLeod–Thomas coaching principles

We have developed a set of coaching principles which we organize into two themed groups: coaching philosophy and coaching dynamics.

Coaching philosophy

- Principles and humanity are more important than skills/tools – while this book is billed as a toolkit, the authors believe wholeheartedly that the principles written here are the bedrock of excellent coaching. The engagement with, and learning from, the principles of coaching are what make coaching work for coachees. The use of tools alone, without the foundation of compassion, service and humility in the coach, leads to clunky, unsatisfactory and unsuccessful outcomes in our view.

- The coach is servant to the coachee; the 'servant' manifests via respect, positive regard, honouring and positivity about outcomes – the notion of the coach as being in the service of the coachee is core to practice in our view. The coach leaves their own agendas, ego **state**s and needs at the door, in pursuit of meeting the coachee's needs. While this does not negate the need for agreements, such contracts themselves serve the client and the outcomes of the coachee and are not for the coach's convenience.

- Humility in the coach creates a graceful openness to learn from the coaching experience – when the coach sees themselves as a partner in the process, it communicates an equality which puts the coachee at ease. Once again, it is the 'ego-less state' of the coach which enables the coachee to progress without hindrance or interference.

- Coaching reveals what is known and unknown and it is the integration of these that creates enough resourcefulness in the coachee for well-being and success. We believe that coaching is a process of 'surfacing and integrating' the experiences, beliefs and awareness of coachees, and it is through accessing these resources within the coachee that the coachee makes most progress. We also believe that a depth of awareness is required which goes well beyond the narrow, single-focus, success goals of the workplace. Coaches wish to have coachees integrate their change to create both success AND well-being in order to produce repeatable, sustainable success.

- The success of the coachee depends upon the coach's ability to quieten their mind and 'get out of the way' (of the process) – coaches need to be able to minimize their own internal chatter and resist the ego-driven desire to advise and fix their coachee. This state of exquisite poise is stimulated by two important qualities. These are being totally engaged with your coachee (in order to serve them) and not allowing your own personal 'stuff' to interfere with their process.

- The coach needs to **facilitate** the widest coachee experiences to harness their motivation and commitment – there can be a tendency in the early experiences of coaches to seize on 'positives' from the coachee and to play down the 'negatives'. It must be recognized that 'polarity' in a coaching session is key to motivating coachees. Polarity involves exploring the light and the dark in a situation, so that the full range of energy can be deployed by the coachee to get started and then to maintain momentum for change and success.

Coaching dynamics

- Exquisite listening, questions, challenges and **silence**s create changes in coachee **perception** – less is more in terms of coaching and the careful and judicious use of **questioning** and challenging, alongside silence, supported by a platform of exquisite listening are key to high quality coaching.

- **Rapport**, within the context of an agreed and maintained relationship creates an effective coaching **dynamic** – rapport is crucial to the relationship as a bedrock for constructive challenges to be offered to the coachee. Contracts and agreements about the expectations of the parties involved are key to that rapport.

- Choices lead to a single sustainable and successful outcome – coaches act to make sure that the coachee has sufficient choices available to them as fuel to their process and progress.

- Self-reflection leads to self-awareness – it's simple, the more you understand about how you function, the more effective you are at self-management.

- The fastest progress is made when the dynamic is fluid and meets the needs of the coachee – we are realists not idealists; we believe that coachees may need a variety of **interventions** in order to succeed and some of the support required may not be coaching. A dynamic exists between coaching and other helping processes such as mentoring and counselling, as well as guidance. An effective coach recognizes the crossing points in conversations between one approach and the next, adapting their support accordingly.

- It's not enough to coach purely to the coachee's targets, one must coach to satisfy targets, wants and needs *in a sustainable way*. This more **holistic** approach to coaching creates success and well-being – echoed in our Coaching Philosophy principles, above. We see well-being as crucial to true success and we advocate coaching which is holistic for an individual in ensuring balance in work, rest and play.

What is right, is it process or instinct?

There is no doubt in our minds that the most outstanding coaches today work instinctively because their competences in the skills and tools that they employ are fully 'installed' – in other words, that they have achieved subconscious competence to a high level, McLeod (2009b: 45). We aver, therefore, that all coaches are best to limit their use of unfamiliar tools to the minimum when working with people. Instead, they are best to rely on a few tools in which they have become totally graceful. That does mean that coaches need to practise their art as much as possible and preferably in a training setting (including, for example, free **co-coaching** arrangements with other coaches). Top international coach, Michelle Duval (2009) says, 'I park my resources, working instinctively' and another leading coach on the world stage, Myles Downey (2009) says, 'Am I consciously using **GROW**? No, but I know that it is present.'

It is not necessary to have 50 tools to be a coach – ultimately, instinct, humanity and principles work magic in managers and leaders at all levels. It is also not necessary to have any knowledge or skills in **neuro-linguistic programming** (NLP). Many disciplines can advise the evolution of intervention-development with a coachee: these include Transactional Analysis,

Emotional Intelligence, **Inner Game** and Servant Leadership. In *The Performance Coaching Toolkit* we have taken, enhanced and created tools from a wide resource of available technology – technologies that we know works fabulously in good hands.

A busy head is not a coaching head. In order to coach, we need to keep our **attention** with the coachee, free from judgements, free from doubts, rehearsal and analyses. Little sparks of genius should arise in the coach and these are triggered by the coachee themselves, not just in words, but in their entire communication system including breathing, posture and other **body language**.

One of the differences between people who call themselves coaches and those who are masterful coaches can be observed in their questioning techniques. From **modelling** analysis of master-classes, the renowned modeller and author, James Lawley (2009), said that McLeod used entirely different questions from those from his previous experiences of modelling 'coaches' in that ALL the questions used by McLeod were very obviously formed with the development of the coachee in mind. All the other 'coaches' were regularly asking questions to inform themselves. This difference is easily accommodated in aspiring master-coaches by setting out with the former objective, rather than the second. Humanity and principles are more important than skills.

Carrots and sticks

Coaching is predicated on the coachee achieving sustainable targets or goals. To achieve motivation for that, the coach will invariably be looking for two sides of every significant 'parcel of communication' in the coachee's experience. In terms of motivation, that means if the coachee is excited about a new pathway to success, that the coach has the discipline to encourage them to delve into what it would be like to fail. In other words, two sets of motivators, so called '**towards**' and '**away-from**' work better than one.

The coach may also take too much for granted in not encouraging other coachee explorations. The coach needs to be a **Devil's Advocate** in seeking out other realities, new perceptions, new choices. All those parcels of communication coming from the coachee may have potential for new growth and energy and there are invariably at least two sides to everything.

Outcomes above targets

Any manager or coach can get excited about a coachee's new target or goal, especially if it seems to be motivating for the coachee. It is important for the coach, as a disciple of best practice, not to get swept along without challenge and exploration to explore the other side of the coachee's motivation. Sometimes an enthusiastic target turns out to be a bad idea. The coach is responsible for sustainable goals, not just motivated ones.

An example of this was a career-coaching session in which the coachee developed an idea to become a helicopter pilot for the paramedic service. The coach was easily swept up by an ambitious prospect, perhaps elevating the coachee to new heights! In fact, when the discipline of looking through the coachee's outcomes was identified, there were several important reasons why the career would very likely be a disaster for the coachee – one of the coachee's outcomes was a wish to develop very close working relationships with others. In fact, by researching the facts of the service in her region, the coachee found that the paramedic pilot was mostly on stand-by, on their own. Mechanics had their own jobs in the workshop, the medics worked as a team and the pilot was outside of that milieu, just a driver, waiting with the aircraft while the medics worked seamlessly at the accident site. Often, the pilot would be sitting alone reading a book, waiting for something to happen.

Issues in coaching relationships: projection

If the coach is predominantly listening, supporting and attending to the needs of the coachee, then there is a good chance that the coach will notice psychological **projection** if it arises. There are two forms of this. One form is where the coach starts to project their own life-map of experience, doubt, hopes and passions. Projection is always driven by emotional need and in this case, the need of the coach. This results in skewed questioning, more an experience of being led, from the observer's perspective, rather than exploratory and supportive. The coachee can be channelled towards a direction that is not right for them and, in serious cases, the coachee may collude with the coach (consciously or subconsciously) to satisfy the coach's need, rather than their own! The problem for the coach is that their own projection will almost certainly be invisible to them. To avoid projection, the coach needs therefore to maintain a disciplined approach to what they do. They also need to set out expectations and boundaries very overtly with the coachee and to make sure that the coachee understands those expectations and boundaries. And the coach must follow through to meet those expectations. The discipline to stay with clean coaching interventions wherever it is helpful will also prevent unwarranted excursions into emotionally-driven projection.

The second form of projection is where the coachee is projecting their own life-map of experience towards the coach. The coachee may, for example, misinterpret the **exquisite attention** of the coach (or the coach's offers of supporting exercises and information) as being a 'special gift' for them alone. On the other hand, the coachee may interpret something the coach says as negative or judgemental and, keeping quiet about that, diminish the prospects for real growth through coaching. In each case, the sensitive, listening coach should have a full awareness of the coachee's communication and always be willing to challenge and express anything that seems to be untoward. For more information on checking methods for projection, see 'projection' in McLeod (2003a: 233).

Issues in coaching relationships: challenge not chat

Colleagues often make poor coaches as they know too much about the coachee and their world. This familiarity can make the coach susceptible so that they flip out of a disciplined **mindset** and into chat mode. The fact is that the most monumental changes in the coachee's psychological state are likely to be generated from challenge. Two reasons why true coaching is so valuable, are: (1) that any individual is limited in their ability to self-challenge; and (2) all of us are nearly incapable of noticing our **patterns**, whether functional (or dysfunctional) to any degree. Challenge takes us out of our **comfort zone** and shakes up our psychology – the skilled human being and coach will be able to challenge and support the coachee through that due to the quality of the coaching relationship. A colleague may find the discipline involved in that process much more difficult to achieve.

Some novice coaches, particularly those coming from an NLP perspective, fail as coaches because one of the four founding pillars of NLP is 'rapport'. A number of such coaches, setting the establishment and maintenance of rapport very high on their set of principles of work, fail to challenge their coachees and so never experience really cathartic change in their charges.

Silence is golden

There are several types of silence and the most important of these is provided as a tool within the main text. However, the value of this type of silence is so enormous that it cannot be omitted here. When a coachee is challenged, the coach should notice any number of a myriad of possible indicators in the coachee. This silence is 'internal processing' silence and is the most self-creative process available to the coachee. The art of the coach is to sit comfortably with that silence and not interrupt it (unless the coachee's psychological state changes again – see text!). These periods of internal processing produce dynamic effects which, at their most monumental, are cathartic. In other words, massive changes in perception, understanding, focus or motivation occur in the coachee, sometimes, all four.

The coaching and managing mix

The **McLeod Management Model** (**MMM**) (2007: 161) (Figure 1.1) advises both managers and coaches when to coach, and when not to! Even in a one-to-one coaching relationship, coaching interventions may sometimes have to be switched off temporarily. Why? Because the coachee does not have enough context, experience and understanding to comprehend either the question or the development step being offered to them by the coach/manager.

Remember that coaching is a facilitative process that does not offer ideas, solutions, instructions, plans or information. Mentoring, on the other hand, is best carried out like coaching (as a predominantly 'facilitated' process) but can include information and ideas ('content') as needed. The indicator for a coachee's need for mentoring is when the coachee does not understand, due to lack of experience or context.

Coaching results in the coachee being enthusiastic and motivated to move forward because they 'own' the solutions. Coaching should also help them think about how to apply any learning in other contexts too. That is another essential job of the professional coach. Coaching will also help them develop their own thinking processes and ability to self-challenge – these two skills help them to be more productive and to have raised well-being and productivity in the longer term. In other words, coaching is helping people to become independently self-starting.

When we look at Figure 1.1, we see a relationship between an individual's degree of 'independence' from their coach/manager and the degree of that same individual's 'self-development'. As someone becomes more self-developed (to the right) so they become more independent from others, their manager or coach (upwards). The context for the whole of the MMM is work but it is also true for any other context since, when we coach, we are not just developing the individual's ability to solve one problem. No, the coach is helping the individual to think smarter *in any context.*

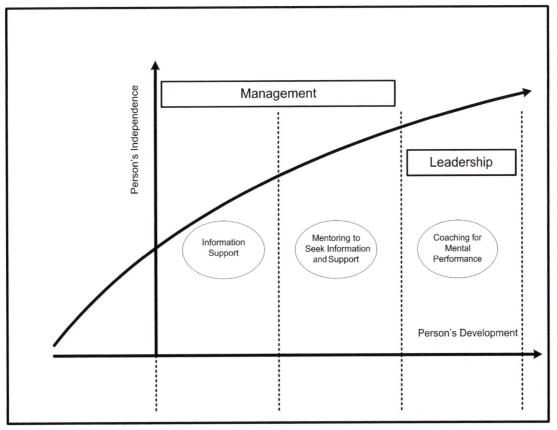

FIGURE 1.1 The McLeod Management Model (MMM)

What the MMM suggests is that, for most adequate people most of the time, we can, as coaches and managers, rely mainly on coaching conversations! When the coachee fails to understand and becomes stuck, the coach switches to mentoring and offers context, choices, knowledge and stories to help move them on. If they are still stuck, then the coach may need to move further to the left of the MMM in Figure 1.1 and provide information, a logical process and/or directions. Once through that, the coach/manager can return to the coaching process (facilitation) once more.

The great benefit of the MMM philosophy is that it encourages coaches and managers to work from the right first – to try facilitative processes in the first instance. In that way, novice coaches, and experienced managers (who are novices in coaching and facilitation) reach the maximum learning experience in their art, every day. The contrary is what typically happens to managers who have learned some new coaching skills in the training room – many go back to work and do what they have always done without changing their style of managing significantly. The MMM model encourages them to start from the right and begin coaching every day. In that way, they gain rapid learning of 'when not to coach' rather than 'when to coach'.

The process of moving from coaching to mentoring, to supporting, and back again is best achieved gracefully. That is, a smooth transition from one style of intervention to the next. For that to happen, the coach/manager needs to be using their skills as much as possible so that they become fluid. The MMM philosophy encourages that learning process.

In Figure 1.1, you will also see some nomenclature for managing and leading. This provides additional context for the model but is not essential to the outcome of the present work.

Further reading

Law, H., Ireland S. and Hussain, Z. (2007) *The Psychology of Coaching, Mentoring and Learning.* Chichester: John Wiley and Sons.

McLeod, A. (2003) *Performance Coaching: The Handbook for Managers, HR Professionals and Coaches.* Carmarthen and New York: Crown House Publishing.

McLeod, A. (2007) *Self-Coaching Leadership: Simple Steps from Manager to Leader.* Chichester: John Wiley and Sons.

Thomas, W. and Smith, A. (2009) *Coaching Solutions: Practical Ways to Improve Performance in Education*, Stafford: Continuum International Press.

Whitmore, J. (2007) *Coaching for Performance.* London: Nicholas Brealey.

The STEPPPA Model

S TEPPPA is an acronym that helps the coach to be sure that the coachee has reached a motivated and sustainable strategy for success. There are a number of steps that appear briefly below:

- **S**ubject – confirming the focus of the discussion and aspects of any contract.

- **T**arget objective – refining a target so that it becomes sustainable.

- **E**motion – developing emotional leverage – ensuring the coachee has enough motivation to commit to, and be sure of, achieving the target.

- **PE**rception – extending choice and increasing the **conscious perception** of the coachee, reframing unhelpful thought patterns.

- **PL**an – developing a realistic process by which the target will be achieved.

- **PA**ce – check that the process developed in the plan is realistic.

- **A**ct/Amend – check that outcomes are satisfied and make a commitment to go ahead.

STEPPPA contains the prime elements of establishing and checking that the strategy will be carried out, will be successful and will enhance the wider context of the coachee's work and life. The steps may be out of order and that is okay, if logical, but every step is important and it may be risky to miss one out completely. Emotion features as a stand-alone item but is also a factor for attention throughout the process. There are other models 'on the market' for coaches, principally GROW and STRIDE. We explore these and compare them with STEPPPA in Chapter 12.

Subject

Coachees work through a variety of issues, whether they are planned or not. The coach needs to check that the subject is one that is permitted within the terms of any contract. The desire of the coachee to get out of the organization may not be an allowable coaching subject, for example. Has the coachee got clarity about the subject of concern? If not, the coach will help them to arrive at a clear understanding.

Target

Very often the coachee also brings a target but is having difficulty in motivating themselves to achieve it (or in having the confidence to decide on the 'best' way of getting there). The coach will already be assessing whether the target is realistic and within the control of the coachee. If not, further questioning will help the coachee arrive at a target that does begin to meet their needs for a **well-formed outcome**. It will also need to fit in with the organizational objectives. Where there is no obvious target expressed by the coachee, the coach will return to this issue after Perception and before Plan.

Emotional context to subject and target

Is the subject something that the coachee has sufficient emotional attachment to want to do anything about it? A question can help, 'Zero to ten, high, how important is it for you to deal successfully with this issue?' Sometimes a coachee may need to reject a subject and do nothing, or simply give the target to someone else. If solving the subject matter does not stimulate, then there is little point in coaching around this issue. If the coachee has an established target objective already, what level of emotional engagement is there with that target objective?

Is their experience of the target ambivalent (mixed)? If it is mixed, then the coach will wish to offer help to the coachee to help extend their understanding of the target objective. That will include emotional aspects, since emotion is critical to motivation. One area to check in this respect is that *personal outcomes* are not unduly compromised by setting out for the target.

Where the coachee has not yet established a really motivating target, the coach will return to its Emotional Context after Perception and before Plan. In any case, the emotional commitment to the final stage will also need to be checked.

Perception and target re-evaluation

Perception is a wonderful key for gaining the coachee's investment in their coach and to assist the coachee in learning how to routinely extend their conscious perception. This process will bring them to a wider and clearer view of the subject and target and provide more choices of action. It is the stage where the coachee may find too many choices. Some will have a better fit for both them and for their organization. At the end of the period of extending and developing conscious perception, the coachee will focus increasingly on targets and strategies that are achievable and exciting.

Plan

The plan will lead to the target. It will be a process, not a series of choices. The coachee may already be motivated to get on with it. The coach will want to encourage the coachee to take a pause in order to check that the target is achievable; that the strategy is feasible within their area of influence and control and that they have considered the wider implications for colleagues, for themselves and for (potentially) their families. Does every element of the coachee's plan accord with corporate policy and the culture of work?

Pace

Pacing will establish whether the target solution has a realistic chance of success and may provide further impetus for achieving it. The contrary is also possible, in which case the target and or the plan may need to be re-worked. Pacing may occur earlier and may even get coached in tandem with planning – a **Time Trail** can achieve this.

Act, amend or commit

It's important to check for any need to adapt the plan before seeking commitment. Once a level of commitment has been established, the coachee will have invested sufficient attention to the subject and target to want to move on. However, the level of motivation is still a 'variable', both rising and falling. The coachee may need to adapt further, perhaps by exposure to some more perceptual work, further attention to vision, beliefs and identity to adjust the plan to achieve a highly motivated coaching result. It is crucial to check the emotional commitment of the coachee and good pacing will have helped. The question, 'zero to ten, high, how certain are you now to achieve your Target by <date/time/>' is also useful.

Further reading

McLeod, A. (2003a) *Performance Coaching: The Handbook for Managers, HR Professionals and Coaches.* Carmarthen and New York: Crown House Publishing.
McLeod, A (2003b) Emotion and coaching, *Anchor Point*, 17(2): 35–41.

2

Coaching Tools

In Part 2, we offer a range of coaching tools organized for clarity into the individual steps of STEPPPA. In addition to these seven elements, we start with an element to act as the bedrock for coaching practice, that of 'foundation'. In this foundation chapter we offer a series of tools that are useful groundwork for coaching and that provide skills and awareness for you as the coach, ideally before you coach professionally.

We have combined the Act/Adapt phase of STEPPPA in one chapter along with the third P of STEPPPA (Pace). Since action follows seamlessly from the STEPPPA process, it seemed natural to combine them. The use of capitalization in the text, for the first and second letters, provides an easy route to recognition and location of tools that relate to each part of the model. In each of the chapters in Part 2 you will find a standard format for presenting the tools, this format consists of:

- Title

- Introduction – contextual information about the tool

- Learning outcomes – learning outcomes for the coachee

- Triggers – common trigger responses from coachees that would warrant use of the tool

- Underpinning rationale – the philosophy or research underpinning the tool

- Instructions for use – a step-by-step guide where needed

- Where do you go from here? – extending the work done with the coachee within and beyond the tool

- Within the tool – notes on any common deviations that coachees tend to make and remedies for those

- Using other tools – linking the tool to other useful tools in the book

- Templates – some tools also have templates that you can copy and use freely with your coachees. These templates are also found on the companion website, available at: www.performancecoachingtoolkit.com.

Foundations of Coaching

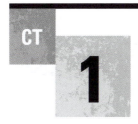

CT

1

The Principal Instruments of Coaching

Introduction

This tool provides a way of reflecting upon your coaching practice or that of others. It asks you to reflect upon the degree to which you use the three principal coaching instruments of Questioning, Silence and Listening. The triangle of instruments (Figure 3.1) gives you a 'ballpark' review and the time-tracker (Table 3.1) gives you the opportunity for someone to tally the time you spend in each of the activities for a more detailed review.

Learning outcomes

Develop a greater awareness of your use of the principal instruments of coaching in yourself and others.

Triggers

- It's about time I reviewed my practice.
- I feel like I am saying too much as the coach.
- I am not making progress with my coachee.

Underpinning rationale

Susan Scott (2002: 218) in her book *Fierce Conversations* suggests 'letting silence do the heavy lifting'. In coaching sessions we can sometimes get out of synchronization with our use of the three principal instruments, this can lead to conversations that stagnate. Too many questions without enough processing time can stifle the coachee's psychological development. Equally, too little coach intervention, when a coachee is genuinely stuck, can also leave them feeling unsupported and wondering why they bothered with coaching. Too much time spent by the coach thinking and formulating their approach and so not spending sufficient time attending to the coachee, can also leave the coach feeling unserved. This tool can create a useful review of the balance between these instruments.

Instructions for use

1   Work with a buddy, using Figure 3.1.

2   Without your buddy seeing this, place a star in the triangle in Figure 3.1 in a position which you believe reflects your current balance of use of the three instruments (Figure 3.2).

3   Have your buddy observe a session. Get them to place a star in the triangle to reflect their perception of your use of the three instruments.

4   Now compare and discuss the two diagrams. Use the key questions in Table 3.1 on p. 21 to assist your discussion.

5   It may be helpful to plan a further observation session where your buddy uses the time-tracker sheet (Table 3.1) to give you more detailed **feedback** and to promote further discussion and action.

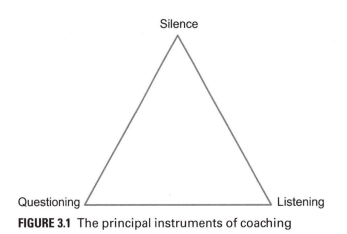

FIGURE 3.1 The principal instruments of coaching

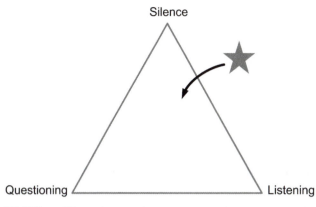

FIGURE 3.2 The principal instruments of coaching, with perception marked

TABLE 3.1 The time-tracker sheet

	Time	Activity	Notes
		Questioning (Q)	
		Listening (L)	
	Start time	*Silence (S)*	
1			
2			
3			
4			
5			
6			
7			
8			
9			
10			
11			
12			
13			
14			
15			

Note: This table is available for download at www.performancecoachingtoolkit.com.

Where do you go from here?

Use the following questions to promote a discussion based on the feedback from your observation:

- What were the strengths of your session?
- When focused on the triangles:
  - What surprises you?
  - How do your two perceptions differ? What might be creating any difference?
  - What beliefs were you running in the session about yourself, and, about your coachee?

○   What was in balance? What was out of balance?
○   What are you learning about your coaching?
○   What needs to change?
○   What actions will you take and when?

Within the tool

Concentrate on the beliefs that are driving your behaviour in the sessions you coach. If there are beliefs that are holding you back, use further tools with your buddy to unblock your path.

Using other tools

Time Trails are worth considering.

2 The Coaching and Mentoring Mix

Introduction

In reality, coaching may have to move to mentoring (to include information, context and other support) depending upon the needs of the coachee in that part of the coaching dynamic.

Learning outcomes

Know how and when to move out of coaching to other types of intervention including mentoring.

Triggers

You have asked a question and the coachee is genuinely so inexperienced, unknowledgeable or has so little contextual understanding of what you have asked, that they cannot move forward in their thinking and experience at that time. This may be accompanied by a gesture of resignation and/or sigh.

Underpinning rationale

Not all coachees will be resourceful, experienced or knowledgeable enough to understand a potentially valuable path forward in their understanding. At those times, they need information, context, **metaphors** or other support to gain enough understanding to take their thinking and experience to a new level. This tool relates to the **McLeod Management Model** (see pp. 10–11, for additional information) (Figure 3.3).

Instructions for use

Use questions, challenge and ensuing silences habitually when coaching, unless the scenario above arises. In that case, prepare to offer context, stores, examples, models and other information to help them to have a more productive comprehension of why and where you are trying to encourage them.

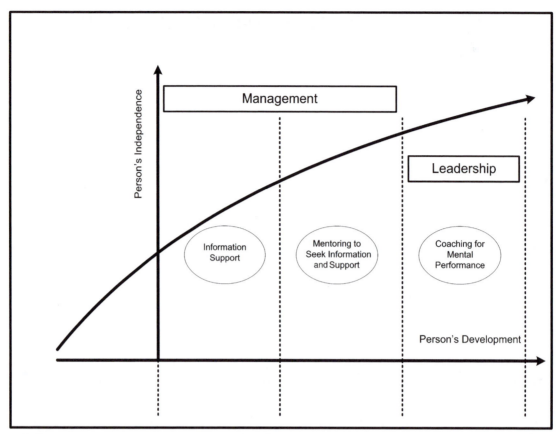

FIGURE 3.3 The McLeod Management Model (MMM)

Where do you go from here?

Within the tool

The coachee will often find that homework that follows on from here and which enhances their learning is helpful. Analyses of what they do, how to make decisions, their values and how these match (or mismatch) their decision are all helpful in this journey. With luck, they will come back with a higher level of learning and commitment in the next session.

Using other tools

The coach may consider the developmental exercise in the principal instruments of coaching tool and also the coach development resource in the **strengths inventory** within the Advanced Tools (Chapter 10).

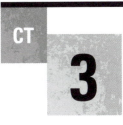

3 Setting up the Space

Introduction

What can you do to enhance the difference between a coaching meeting and any other type of meeting? We provide some thoughts to help you.

Learning outcomes

Know what is important and why.

Triggers

Pre-session preparation for a coaching-style dialogue.

Underpinning rationale

Coaching is a supporting, facilitation methodology and the setting up of the space and the coach's part in that space are important in stimulating the behaviours that support and underpin the founding principles of coaching best practice.

Instructions for use

Your session space should have the following:

Local toilets, available fire exit, be closed off from possible onlookers and listeners, have phones that can be unplugged or turned off, have no table or, if it does, a corner that can be used for the first part of the session. Also, at least three chairs – all identical. Ideally, make sure that there is enough space to move around in case you need to offer **time trails**, **Perceptual Position**s and **Resourceful Space**s. Prepare a notice for the door to prevent interruptions. Ensure that the room is comfortable for light and temperature needs. Provide a source of clean water. Check that there is a flipchart, pens, notepads and coloured pens for either of you to use.

If the coach arrives first, make sure that neither you nor your effects 'take ownership' over any of the seating choices or any work surface associated with those possible seat choices. We are trying to create an egalitarian space where the coach offers first choice of 'ownership' to the coachee.

Where do you go from here?

The early setting up of coaching gives way to the dialogue for change. This can be supported through the STEPPPA process, outlined in Part 2 of this book.

Within the tool

Enhancements of the tool would include a means of fixing flip-charts to the walls. Also, cards or self-adhesive stickers to write on, as well as other writing and drawing media may be useful. A round table is better for preference. A bigger room offering the possibility of walking a 6-metre time trail, will allow more flexibility and also be more useful should the coachee want to take Tool PE8 the **Third Perceptual Position** or wish to move to a resourceful position, some distance from where they are already situated. See also the following tools:

Tool CT4 Setting up the Session
Tool CT7 Clean Language
Tool PE9 The **51% Rule**.

CT

4 Setting up the Session

Introduction

Having worked on the space for the session, what is the most effective way of building rapport? This tool assumes that pre-session contractual communication explaining expectations (see Part 3) has already been distributed and seen. This is best checked out before the session.

Learning outcomes

- Understand that the journey of the coaching process is also with the coachee.
- Knowing when and how to start the actual coaching work.

Triggers

Meeting the coachee for the first session or any subsequent session.

Underpinning rationale

- Not all coachees are immediately ready to enter the work of a session.
- The coachee's need for rapport and a working level of trust is an individual journey.
- The coachee is best to decide when to start 'work'.
- If you establish that the level of risk-taking is within their control, the coachee will usually prepare psychologically for greater levels of expression and risk.

Instructions for use

A systematic approach might include the following steps summarized by the acronym 'MISS B' (see Table 3.2).

TABLE 3.2 Setting up a session using MISS B

Action	Information or method
Meet	Introductions, normal chit-chat, show interest, discuss sports news, for example, avoid politics
Invite	Where do they want to sit (see Tool CT3 Setting up the Space)?
Space	Suggest that some people have further questions or want to know more about their coach or coaching process before moving into the process itself – invite them to ask also
State	Overtly check their psychological state for coaching, ask 'So, zero to ten, how ready are you to make a start?' and possibly, 'What do you/we need to do to improve that now?'
Begin	Ask, 'So, do you have an issue or target that you would like to work with?'

Where do you go from here?

Work through the STEPPPA model (Chapter 2) to develop learning and action steps with the coachee.

Within the tool

It is important to watch for signs of discomfort and to check out the apparent ease (or lack of ease) of the coachee. You can do this verbally by asking, 'How confident and relaxed are you now, zero to ten?' and, 'With that level of confidence and relaxation, what would be the most fruitful and perhaps risky thing that you might work on now?'

Other useful phrases

'You can choose how much risk to take here and it is not important for me to know whether that is a small, medium or big risk for you, as only you will know. A small risk for you might be big for me and vice versa.' This presupposes that that there will be risk and so raises the potential for risk at the higher level.

'Okay, so you have not brought an issue or target with you this first time, so why not tell me, if you will, what is going well for you, in a nutshell, and what is going less well for you now?' They will most likely be aware of what you are doing. Talking about their successes first will allow them to become more comfortable with you. It will also give them more space to prepare themselves psychologically (to deal with the second half of the question).

Using other tools

Look at other tools such as Tool PE9 the 51% Rule and Tool CT5 Body Clues.

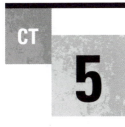

5 Body Clues

Introduction

B ody clues help the coach to notice both the coachee's psychological state and whether they are being authentic (see **Authenticity**) in what they say. Body clues also provide information related to the degree of psychological **association** or **dissociation** that the coachee has with the material being expressed by them, see Tool E3 Associated and Dissociated States.

Learning outcomes

Notice coachee changes in state, posture and voice.

Triggers

The following triggers for noticing Body Clues might be observed:

- A mismatch in energy in the physical 'being' of the person and what energy might be expected from the words they are saying.
- Repeated movement (for example, a tic).
- Changes in muscle tone and skin pallor.
- Changing their posture.

Underpinning rationale

- Changes in individual energy provide clues to a person's psychological state.
- Body clues can indicate a possible mismatch between what is said and what is 'experienced' by the coachee.
- Repeated movements (tics and twitches) are often the result of 'psychological leakage' and provide clues that the coachee may be struggling emotionally.

Instructions for use

Increase your levels of awareness of inauthentic physical and verbal communication. Your awareness can be enhanced by using peripheral vision to observe the coachee – the coach does not have to stare at their coachee! It involves looking at them directly and then softening the focus of your eyes to include the peripheral aspects of the room you are in. In this 'peripheral vision state' you will be able to notice a wider range of changes in the coachee's behaviours than might be observable in more direct (foveal) observation (Figure 3.4). You may notice some of the following mismatches occurring with your coachee:

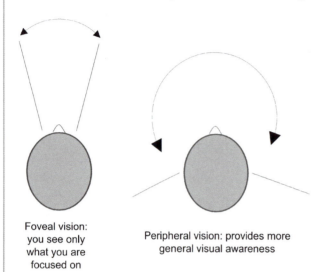

Foveal vision: you see only what you are focused on

Peripheral vision: provides more general visual awareness

FIGURE 3.4 Fields of awareness

1   'I think I can really do this now' but said with a monotonous or low voice, slumped posture.

2   'It's not a problem' but accompanied by the start of eyelid twitches or eye movements, finger tapping or dropping of the shoulders.

3   'I honestly do not care about them' associated with blood-colouring or draining, or blotching in the neck.

In the same order, the coach's responses might include the following:

1   Do you think you can do this now or can you do this now? And if you could look at yourself saying that <mimics> 'I think I can really do this now', like that, would you believe in you?

2   Is that how <mimics> 'It's not a problem' looks? Calibrate 'not a problem' for me. How much is it not a problem?

3   Is there another word for how you think or feel about them?

A repeated tic could simply mean that a coachee needs the bathroom! It may also mean that they have some emotional discomfort with the subject they are experiencing internally at that point. This might be anger, anxiety, fear, internal conflict, feeling pushed or a myriad of other emotionally-based experiences. A typical response by the coach might be: 'I get the feeling that you are not fully content when talking about this. If that were true, and I am not saying that it is true, in what way are you not fully content?'

Where do you go from here?

Within the tool

Be prepared to draw attention to **incongruent** physical and verbal clues, for example, 'I notice your voice is slow and your head dropped a little as you said that you were excited about the goal.' Await a response to your observation or question it further. You might go on to question for a root cause for that behaviour. 'And if there was something behind that, what is that something now?'

Using other tools

Within the tool, using Tool CT7 Clean Language can be helpful. Developing a clearer picture of the challenges that a coachee faces, can be achieved using the Tool S3 Wheel of Work. Tool S4 the Motivation Teaser can assist coaches to understand the motivational drivers of their coachees, and consequently to help the coach to adjust language to meet the needs of their coachee.

CT

6 Reflective Language

Introduction

Reflective language is used to show the coachee that you are listening. It is used to allow the coachee to explore their psychological experience without the need to pause (and logically question) what the coach *means* when the coach uses different words to their own (with potentially different semantic meaning). It allows the coachee to 're-hear' their own words and to clarify meaning for themselves.

Learning outcomes

- Understand why reflective language is important in coaching.
- Know how to up-skill in the technique.

Triggers

Use reflective language frequently in coaching, particularly when summarizing. The coach will also need to use reflective language when the coachee is exploring, processing and sharing that exploration or processing in words. You may need to stop using reflective language in a situation in which the coachee is distressed (and their psychological state needs to be less emotional and more resourceful).

Underpinning rationale

- What the coachee says, exactly, can be 'heard' by them without need for conscious processing, unless it conflicts with their values.

- This psychological phenomenon is due to the natural creation of **neural pathways** (in the brain). These neural pathways are sometimes referred to as 'keys to the unconscious' (Figure 3.5).

- When used successfully, coachees are mostly unaware of the repetitive nature of the sentences or the contrived nature of the complex uses of reflective language.

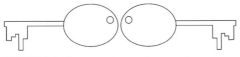

FIGURE 3.5 Keys to the subconscious

Instructions for use

Start by using key words or phrases in your responses and questions. If you struggle to recall the word or phrase, simply replace it with the word 'that'. Combine the phrase with precise use of grammatical structure and tense.

Coachee 1: When I have that experience it is like a rush of tingling up and down my neck and back.

Coach So you experience this tingling up and down <pause> and as you experience this tingling up and down, what else are you noticing?

Coachee 2: Margaret was really upset and had a go at me and all because she was stressed because of the monthly management report – and it is nothing to do with me! All I needed were some figures to complete my own report. She was out of order. Bruce said so too and he was just outside sorting some papers for the opening event. I felt battered. Bruce said that I should go over her head to the MD and get her to sort her out. I would have, but the MD has been on leave and so over a week has gone by.

Coach : So when you felt like that, and if you could say something honest to her now, what is it you would like to say to her now, as you feel like that?

Coachee 3: I can't be bothered with him.
Coach : So when you can't be bothered with him, what else are you aware of?

Where do you go from here?

Within the tool

Practise using reflective words and phrases rather than long sentences. In time, you will be able to select short passages of words that are most significant. Some people think that reflective language could be annoying, but that will only be the case if it is done badly. The whole point of reflective language is that the coachee is rarely aware of it; it helps suspend them in that same psychological state – where the words flow in without analysis.

Using other tools

Reflective language forms the core skill that underpins all processes for maintaining psychological state in the coachee. Look at Tool CT7 Clean Language which also maintains state.

7 Clean Language

Introduction

David Grove developed a series of questions called **clean language** that reflect much of the coachee's language back to them. These language patterns minimize the interference between the coach's 'model of the world' and the 'world view' belonging to the coachee. Consequently, the coachee is able to think in a coaching environment where there are few, if any, prejudices, or 'foreign' insights. Lawley and Tompkins (2000: 86), who studied Grove over several years, found that he used a series of just nine basic questions for *most* of his coaching interventions. This tool offers an **aide-mémoire** for coaches to use these nine clean language questions. They are provided in the form of a bookmark which can be cut out, laminated and held on the lap (or pinned to a pad) during a session.

Learning outcomes

● Have the nine, basic, clean questions ready to hand (Appendix 1).
● Practise and embed the nine basic clean language questions.

Triggers

Any metaphor or **analogy** offered by the coachee, for example:

Coachee: I am feeling swamped by the demands placed on me at the moment.
Coach: And what kind of swamped is that swamped?

Any situation where it might be useful for the coachee to create a new, coachee-generated, metaphorical view of that situation.

Underpinning rationale

Less interference in a coachee's model of **reality** leads to coachee solutions that are more authentically 'theirs'. The self-determination created by clean language is highly motivating and leaves the coachee firmly in control of their problems and solutions.

Instructions for use

1   Use the aide-mémoire in any situation where there is a metaphor, analogy, or simile to explore or where ownership of the problem and the solution needs heightening.

2   Feed the coachee's language into the most appropriate clean language question.

3   Be ready to follow up the question with another from the list.

Where do you go from here?

Within the tool

Use the questions so you can facilitate the coachee to their solution. Stick to clean language, remembering that the process needs to be going on in your coachee's head, not yours. Resist the temptation to lead with comments, **affirmation**s or leading questions. Sit back and watch the magic happen.

Using other tools

Consider Tool PE7 Perceptual Positions – the **Second Position** and Tool PE1 Objective Advice.

Tenses

Introduction

Precise use of past, present and future tenses can either help to shift awareness or help the coachee to explore an uninterrupted, psychological experience that may be helpful in motivating them towards, or away from, that experience. Tenses can also be used to help associate or dissociate to/from emotions (more later).

Learning outcomes

- Why tenses are important.
- When to employ tense patterns.

Triggers

- I was successful then.
- I don't like doing . . .
- I am terrible at . . .

Underpinning rationale

We tend to be more psychologically associated with things we speak about in the *present* tense. If these are non-productive, then moving that experience into the past (using past tense) can open the possibility of creating 'permission' for change. It is helpful for people to have two distinct types of reference experiences: ones that are current, unpleasant reactions to a stimulus and ones that have reference experiences that are pleasant (and that could replace the unpleasant experience with further coaching).

Instructions for use

Capital letters denote tense only and not the actual time being discussed at that moment, thus, PA = Past tense, PR = Present tense, and F = Future tense. Resourcing may refer to the past or the future (in order to get a starting point for the coachee), but will in each case be moved into the *present* tense in order to bring their emotional resources, from those other times, into a real experiencing, in the present.

Example 1

Coachee: I was successful then. (PA)
Coach: Could you be successful now? (PR)
Coachee: I could, but need more confidence.
Coach: You could be more successful now but need more confidence? So, can you have that confidence of being successful again here and now, as if you already have enough confidence to be successful now? (resourcing PR)
Coachee: Yes, I am doing that (PR) but it is coming and going.
Coach: So if there is something else that helps that confidence to stay longer and you are more successful, what is that something that helps now? (PR)
Coachee: Breathing out, relaxing.
Coach: And so as you breathe out and relax, you are more confident and successful? (PR)
Coachee: That's right.

Example 2

Coachee: I don't like doing reports. (PR)
Coach: Have you ever had an experience of liking doing all or part of a report?
Coachee: Sometimes the middle bits, but not starting or reading over and over again to make it scan better.
Coach: So you mainly have not liked doing reports up until now? But sometimes you have liked doing the middle bits?
Coachee: Yes.
Coach: So you can enjoy doing part of a report now (PR) or in the future?
Coachee: Yes, sometimes.
Coach: So what good experience of writing a report would you like to have next time? Imagine the clock is spinning forward, hours and days moving, and there is another report for you now, what it is like having this report now? (resourcing PR)
Coachee: I feel better about the middle and I have just sketched out the start rather than plodding through it, so I can now complete the middle, which makes it easier to revisit the start and complete the conclusions. (PR)
Coach: So having this report and having sketched out the start and completed the middle, what is this experience like now? (PR)
Coachee: It's great, much better. (PR)
Coach: So, the clock is spinning back, here we are, it's Tuesday and I make it ten past three, do you? And here we are in this room and I can hear a heavy vehicle passing by outside. Knowing and experiencing what you experienced in the future, is there a difference? (resourcing PR)
Coachee: Yes, it is down to my attitude and approach. (PR)

Example 3

Coachee: I am terrible at talking in board meetings. (PR)
Coach: Always?
Coachee: Not always.
Coach: So, sometimes you were terrible or less terrible, or something else at board meetings?
Coachee: I am mostly terrible, sometimes less so. (PR)
Coach: So if we go back to a recent meeting where you are 'less than terrible', what is this 'less than terrible' like; what do we notice about you? (resourcing PR)
Coachee: I am going red in the face, I am speaking (PR), but afterwards realize that I should have said more.
Coach: So you realize that you should have said more (PR). Do you ever have better experiences than this?
Coachee: Not much, this is about as good as it gets.
Coach: So let's look at this from the perspective of this room and this session. So, here we are talking about your experiences of being 'less than terrible', can you refer to that in a more positive way? (PR)
Coachee: My managing way.
Coach: Would it be helpful to understand more about your 'managing way' and maybe to see if you can do more or less of certain aspects of your 'managing way' in order to create another and even better experience of talking at board meetings?

Where do you go from here?

Within the tool

Continue to use tense as required.

Using other tools

Consider Tool PE5 Leader and Follower, Tool E4 **Anchoring**, Tool PE10 **SWISH**, and sensory journeys. See also Emotions (Chapter 6) and to help associate or dissociate emotions appropriately.

9 STEPPPA – Quick Prompt

This tool acts as a very quick prompt for structuring a coaching session. The STEPPPA coaching model provides a structure to assist you both during coaching and afterwards, when reflecting upon your coaching practice. It provides a set of questions to stimulate discussion and insight during coaching sessions. The STEPPPA model has the following stages, although they are not necessarily linear (p. 13). For more information about STEPPPA and how to use it, see Chapter 1, the Coaching and Managing Mix (pp. 10–11).

- **S**ubject – confirming the focus of the discussion and aspects of any contract.
- **T**arget objective – refining a target so that it becomes sustainable.
- **E**motion – developing emotional leverage – ensuring the coachee has enough motivation to commit to, and be sure of, achieving the target.
- **PE**rception – extending choice and increasing the conscious perception of the coachee, reframing unhelpful thought patterns.
- **PL**an – developing a realistic process by which the target will be achieved.
- **PA**ce – check that the process developed in the plan is realistic.
- **A**ct/**A**dopt – check that outcomes are satisfied and make a commitment to go ahead.

Learning outcomes

The tool provides:

- Quick prompt questions for each stage of the coaching process.
- A reflective-practice prompt sheet to consider the content and process of a recorded conversation in order to enhance a coach's skills.
- A helpful record of coaching progress, in steps, for coaches and coachees.

Triggers

Any coaching situation.

Underpinning rationale

Having a model like STEPPPA is not essential for all coaches, but is particularly helpful in early and intermediate coaching. The expert coach will have a wide repertoire of questions and other intervention skills and will be completely at ease with those. This degree of expertise makes it more likely the coach will be effective in the service of the coachee. Even seasoned coaches can benefit from the use of a framework to refer to, if progress is not being made with a coachee or where the coach wishes to reflect upon their practice. This can be beneficial both for themselves and for teaching others.

Instructions for use

Use the STEPPPA prompt sheet as a prompt for questioning or as a reflective-practice grid. Treat it as a checklist of appropriateness rather than a prescriptive and sequenced list. In other words, you don't necessarily have to conduct a session in this order, nor use all of the questions. We encourage you to use this sheet as a prompt, and then to let your active listening skills generate further, curious questions.

STEPPPA Coaching Prompt Sheet

Date:	Session ____ of ____

Discussion between _____ and _____

Time: _____ Duration: _____ Location: _____

Discussion focus/Follow-up from previous session:

Actions agreed previously:

Session record for today

	NOTES:
Subject: What do you want to focus on? What do you want to change? **Target:** What do you want as an outcome from this session? What do you want as mid- and long-term outcomes in this area of your life/work? **Emotion:** What excites you about this target? How will you know when you have achieved this target specifically? **Perception:** What are you choosing here? What other choices are there? What strengths do you have that could help you here? What could you do if you did not have to live with the results of your actions? **Plan:** From your options, which is the quickest/easiest/cheapest/most comfortable/least comfortable/most effective thing to do? What feels right here? What will you do first? . . . second? . . . next? . . . then? **Pace:** When will you take these steps? How realistic is this course of action you have chosen? When will you review your progress towards your target? **Amend/Act:** How realistic is your plan? What if anything might you need to adjust to make this happen? What will you do? When will you do it? **ACTIONS AGREED/QUESTIONS TO CONSIDER:**	 **NEXT MEETING:**

Where do you go from here?

Within the tool

Initially, use the prompt for your coaching sessions and then consider changing the questions in the grid for alternatives which have the same effect, but which are more authentic to your style of speaking.

Using other tools

Expand your repertoire of questions with the STEPPPA Question Bank (Appendix 2). If you wish to extend or deepen understanding for the coachee, consider plucking tools from the relevant chapter of Part 2 of this book to extend the coachee experience. For example, if you want the coachee to plan more deeply, pick a tool like Tool PL1 Logical Wheels from Part 2.

10 STEPPPA Coaching Matrix

Introduction

A flow chart is available for the early use of the STEPPPA coaching model (Figure 3.6). It is ideal for practising your coaching process and for reviewing it.

Learning outcomes

- Get a feel for the way that a coaching conversation moves back and forth through the STEPPPA model.
- Analyse your practice through using the flow chart to assess your coaching practice (e.g. by watching a video of your practice).

Triggers

You wish to further enhance your coaching practice through the structuring of the coaching dialogue.

Underpinning rationale

Although the conscious use of structures like STEPPPA become less important when your coaching skills develop, it can be useful to analyse your coaching practice using a flow chart. This is not to say that the flow chart is always right, but more that it provides a pathway which you can reflect upon and compare against your live practice. Working with a buddy for this is particularly valuable.

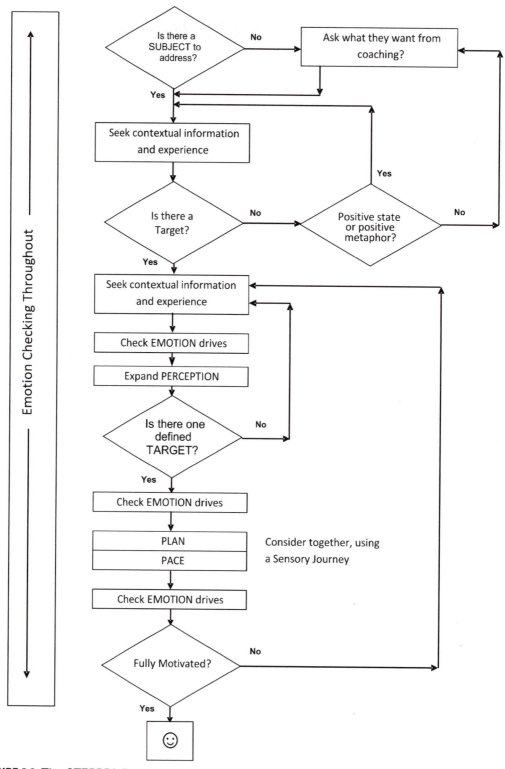

FIGURE 3.6 The STEPPPA flow chart

Note: This figure is downloadable at www.performancecoachingtoolkit.com.

Instructions for use

1   Have a colleague observe your coaching, or video your session.

2   Watch your session on the tape, or use the notes and observations from your colleague alongside the flow chart to generate a discussion about the way you move around the different aspects of the coaching conversation.

3   Use the following reflection questions to promote discussion:
   (a)   Where do you match the flow chart?
   (b)   Where do you differ from it?
   (c)   What are the effects upon the coachee?
   (d)   Were there any omissions or additional steps not highlighted by the flow chart?
   (e)   What was intuitive and what was conscious about your coaching process?

Where do you go from here?

Within the tool

The possibilities for Tool CT6 Reflective Language practice are endless with such a tool as this. You may wish to develop a deeper understanding of the overview of your use of STEPPPA or you might choose to focus on a specific aspect of the model, for example, how you suitably engage the emotions of the coachee.

Using other tools

Any tool in Part 2 of this book will fit into the development of your own coaching once you identify your specific development needs.

Further reading

Downey, M. (2003) *Effective Coaching*. London: Texere.
Landsberg, M. (1996) *The Tao of Coaching*. London: HarperCollins Business.
Lawley, J. and Tompkins, P. (2000) *Metaphors in Mind*. London: The Developing Company Press.
McDermott, I. and Jago, W. (2003) *The NLP Coach*. London: Piatkus.
McLeod, A. (2003) *Performance Coaching: The Handbook for Managers, HR Professionals and Coaches*. Carmarthen and New York: Crown House Publishing.

CHAPTER 4

Subject Focus in STEPPPA

S1 Pattern Breaker

Introduction

Both thinking and behavioural patterns that are *not* helpful to the coachee may be broken, using this tool.

Learning outcomes

When and how to apply Tool S1 **Pattern Breaker**.

Triggers

- And then I drive faster and with more aggression.
- The voice in my head says 'NO!'

Underpinning rationale

Patterns of thought and behaviour are learned automatically. They are learned as a result of specific and repeated stimuli. They then recur due to that single stimulus. Interrupting the pattern can often lead to a new and more useful experience. This new experience can be **anchored** and so create a new, and automatic response to the same stimuli in the future.

Instructions for use

1   Identify the external trigger.

2   Identify the earliest part of their internal response, in terms of their experience and/or thinking.

3   Isolate one significant interrupter to change that experience or thought.

4   Ask them to rehearse the situation using the interrupter.

The trigger is the external stimulus that creates the learned response in them. Example questions to use that follow on from the above triggers are:

> So, what is it that happens that makes you drive faster and with more aggression?
> And when the voice in your head says 'NO!', what is it that caused that?

The earliest part of their response to the trigger may or may not be the reaction that they have described to you, for example 'The voice in my head says NO!' So, question to check:

> And when that happens and the voice in your head says 'NO', if there is there anything else you notice just before the voice says 'NO!', what is that something else you notice?

The interrupter will typically be something of their own choosing, but they may need some examples if they are struggling to think of something. In this situation, some people pinch themselves in a particular way, or they have a loud statement in their heads that says, 'WHO SAYS "NO"?!' The rehearsal will help them to anchor a new response to the trigger.

Where do you go from here?

Within the tool

If it is working, ask them to imagine a recurring time in the future and see if it is still effective. If not, consider inviting the coachee to rehearse the different psychological states again, as perfectly as possible, and then try again.

Using other tools

Sensory journeys and Tool PL2 Time Trail can also be useful tools in encouraging rehearsal and emotional engagement with new patterns of thought or behaviour. Equally, adding Tool AT1 Totems and Archetypes to behaviours can be beneficial.

2 Value Discovery Tool

Introduction

The emergence of a coachee's clear understanding of their personal values (what is important to them) is the basic foundation for them making decisions and setting goals that will meet their needs. This activity is a powerful way of helping people who find themselves in conflict when making a decision. It is a great activity for them to do as homework and to bring to the next coaching session.

The activity can be repeated as if the coachee was replying 'for their organization' and had the values of that organization in their mind at the time. The similarities and differences (the gaps) can be highly useful learning material. It can help an individual to identify why particular aspects of an organization cause them anxiety and stress. For individuals who are in conflict with aspects of the institution, other individuals or 'the system', this work can help them to resolve those differences. Raising conscious awareness, personal values and organizational values and exploring the common ground, all help to reduce conflict. Exploring the differences in values and then looking at what is similar about those differences can help resolve real conflict – sounds strange, but it works!

Learning outcomes

- What we mean by a 'value'.
- How to develop an accurately ranked list of a coachee's values.
- How to use values as a basis for decision-making and analysing any gaps between present and desired thoughts, feelings and behaviours.

Triggers

Coachees may say:

> How do I know which is the right option for me?
> I am not sure what is right for me.
> I have a dilemma.

Similarly, coaches may want to understand what is most highly valued by an individual, so that they can gauge and probe potentially inauthentic responses.

Underpinning rationale

The tool works by bringing to the coachee's conscious awareness those things that are important to them (their values). It gets them to create a hierachy of values. It allows people to reflect upon why certain aspects of tasks, other people and organizations can annoy us, while others do not. The tool can be used to provide coachees with a decision-making prompt for key dilemmas. Matching decision options to the list of values can assist in making a decision.

Instructions for use

Look at Value Discovery 1 and Value Discovery 2. You will need ten strips of card available for the sorting process.

Value Discovery 1

What are values?

A value is something you naturally feel is important to you. There is a difference between wants, needs and values: a value is something you are drawn to and is not influenced by your wants and needs. Following your values helps you set better goals. When your goals are in line with your values, you feel happier and your goals are easier to achieve. Doing the activity below can seriously improve your happiness!

Getting to know your own values

To begin with, Table 4.1 shows some examples of values that some people have identified in the past in relation to their work. These are just examples – your values are *your* values and no one can make them up for you.

TABLE 4.1 Examples of common values

adventure	competition	community
collaboration	detail	understanding
fairness	flexibility	freedom
fun	perfection	money
health	honesty	independence
integrity	knowledge	learning
order	power	friendship

Value Discovery 2

1   Make a list of personal values – the question to ask to find a value is: 'What is important to me?' Remember these are not wants or needs, they are simply things you feel are important to you.

2 When you have about ten values, write them onto cards (one on each card). Begin to arrange them in order of priority, with the most important at the top and the least important at the bottom. Do this quickly and use your 'gut feelings'. The idea is to get an approximate order of importance. The next step is to refine your list.

3 Now, starting at the second value, take each value and test it against both the one above and the one below it. Ask the question: 'Is this value really more important than the one below and less important than the one above?' Move cards as necessary to fine-tune your priority list.

4 Repeat this process until you are happy with your values priority list.

5 Once you are happy with your list, copy the hierarchy into the value discovery table.

6 Now, trusting your 'gut feeling' again, score each value between 1 and 5 based on how well you are currently living by that value (in your life as a whole). Five represents fully living by the value and 1 not really living by it. Record the value in the third column of Table 4.2. As you do this, note down in the fourth column any feelings or thoughts that come to you as you do the activity

7 Now, consider Table 4.2 and its contents using these questions:
   (a) What are my strengths?
   (b) Where in my work am I living by my values?
   (c) Where am I living by my values least?
   (d) What happens when I am living to my values? (as in question b)
   (e) And, when I am not living by my values? (as in question c)
   (f) What strikes me about what I put in column 4?
   (g) What am I learning about myself?

TABLE 4.2 Value discovery sheet

Priority ranking	Value	Living by this value	Feelings/thoughts
1			
2			
3			
4			
5			
6			
7			
8			
9			
10			

Note: This table is available for download at www.performancecoachingtoolkit.com.

Where do you go from here?

Within the tool

Keep a list of the coachee's top values close at hand and encourage them to do so too. Whenever there is conflict or low motivation in the coachee, encourage them to go back to the list and to find ways of achieving their goals by being sympathetic or 'in line' with those values. With some creative questioning you can usually build bridges between conflicting values; at least enough to soften hardened attitudes.

Repeating the activity every three to six months is valuable and often reveals useful learning. The values approach can also be used to identify strengths and lead into development areas for setting targets and for exploring the reality of real situations with increased clarity.

The coachee may present with various degrees of willingness to engage with this activity and your skills of rapport building and timing will allow you to judge the best time to invite the person you are coaching to do this. Similarly, the degree of disclosure can be left to the individual by setting it as a homework task, and being clear that they can choose what they want to share.

Carrying out the activity for perceptions of *another person's* values or those of an organization can help people to further understand any internal conflict.

Using other tools

Try both Tool PE7 Second and Tool PE8 Third Position, Tool PE2 Authenticity Profile, and Tool T1 Well-formed Outcome.

3 The Wheel of Life and the Wheel of Work

Introduction

The Wheel of Work and the Wheel of Life are both useful tools at the beginning of a coaching/managing relationship. They provide high-quality information about how the coachee experiences their world of life or work, and how they want it to be. They provide a rich resource for potential, coachee-led targets.

Learning outcomes

Understanding best practice in using the wheels.

Triggers

The start of a coaching relationship is most typical.

Underpinning rationale

The tools both manage the gaps between 'current' experiences and 'desired' experiences and establish the facilitation qualities of the coaching relationship. They additionally provide a joint focus for work between the coach and coachee. They also provide physical proximity (it is an activity to carry out side-by-side) and this comfortable, working proximity can help establish more trust (in relation to the coachee's 'personal space').

Instructions for use

Two wheels, one for life-coaching and one designed for work are both provided (Figures 4.1 and 4.2). Whichever one your coachee decides to use, explain the wheel, its purpose and then seek permission to explore it. Say to them, 'For each segment in the wheel, ask yourself "how content am I from zero to ten?", where ten is about as good as it could be – start anywhere you like.' Then, ask, 'For each segment, where can you realistically improve things and to what level, zero to ten, and over what time scale?' Ask, 'Some people find it useful to identify the greatest gaps between how things are now and how they want things to improve over time. Could you do that and talk through your perceptions about how you may manage those gaps and make a difference?'

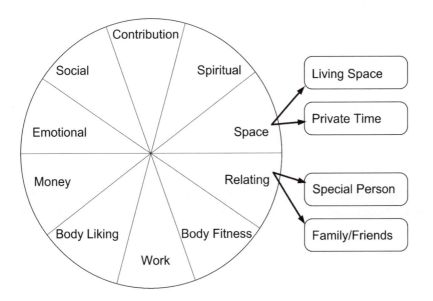

FIGURE 4.1 The wheel of life
Note: This figure is downloadable at www.performancecoachingtoolkit.com.

FIGURE 4.2 The wheel of work
Note: This figure is downloadable at www.performancecoachingtoolkit.com.

Where do you go from here?

Within the tool

Where an individual scores all their aspirations quite low, ask a supplementary question, 'I notice your aspirations are all marked below six and wonder if six is as high as you would ever score each of those – in other words, is your six someone else's nine or ten?' If they reply that they never score anything above a (say) seven, this prevents the coach from persisting in pushing towards higher scores (that for the coachee are anyway adequate and realistic). Ask them to make priorities for coaching: 'Some people find it useful to identify two or three issues or targets for a series of coaching sessions, would you like to choose, say, one big issue for you and one or two smaller issues or goals?'

Using other tools

The STEPPPA Quick Prompt (pp. 39–42) will help to begin the coaching process. Also Tool T1 the Well-formed Outcome to create targets in each area of the wheel that the coachee may then develop.

4 Motivation Teaser

Introduction

This tool supports a coachee to better understand what motivates and de-motivates them, by teasing out factors that energize or inhibit their performance. It can be used conversationally with a coachee within a session or it can be offered as a stimulating task for coachees to complete between coaching sessions.

Learning outcomes

- Coachees learn what their key motivators are.
- Coachees also learn what de-motivates them.
- It offers the opportunity for re-invigorating roles, tasks, and processes by understanding more of what they need to do and what they need to avoid on their path to success.

Triggers

Coachees might say:

- I just can't get excited about X.
- I get so frustrated by Y.
- No matter how hard I try, I can't improve in this area.

Underpinning rationale

By enabling coachees to understand the motivators and de-motivators in the context of their work, they can be empowered to manage their tasks in more fulfilling ways. Their creativity can be encouraged in approaching aspects of their role which have been de-motivating – to bring in more of their motivational drivers. The process also allows them to make judgements about the 'fit' of their role to their skills, knowledge, beliefs and values.

Instructions for use

1 Introduce the coachee to the idea of motivators and de-motivators. Motivators are personal factors which energize and drive a person towards action and completion. De-motivators trigger un**resourceful state**s of mind (e.g. apathy, anxiety, and boredom), which inhibit action and completion.

2 Explain that you are going to offer the coachee a series of questions which will help them to be more consciously aware of their motivators and de-motivators. Explain also that they will get even more benefit from this exercise if they trust their first instinctive responses.

3 Take them through the tool, or offer the tool to work on between sessions.

Where do you go from here?

Within the tool

If you use the question: 'And what else?', it enables the coachee to search for factors beyond the initially accessible thoughts. Allow processing time, and observe your coachee for signs of genuine completion versus 'still thinking'. Try the question, 'So, what does that do for you?' Then explore with the coachee:

- how they could turn de-motivators into motivators or use de-motivators in positive ways, for example, to relax or to overcome boredom;

- how they could maximize the use of their motivators to overcome any de-motivating factors in a specific area of their work;

- the range of choices they have for dealing with each de-motivator.

Using other tools

Any de-motivators that cause particularly difficult emotional conflicts for a coachee can be dealt with using the Conflict Resolution and Integration tool (Table 4.3).

Begin with your key motivators. List in the first column everything that motivates you. Then in the second column list everything that de-motivates you. Keep adding to the list until you run out of thoughts. Ask the question, 'and what else?' to extend your thinking.

Once you have listed all of the motivators and de-motivators you can think of, move on to the following questions to assist you in eliciting more subconscious help with motivators/de-motivators. Add any new factors into the appropriate columns in Table 4.2.

- What frustrates my performance?

- To what extent do the changes being made/(that have been made) affect me or my colleagues?

TABLE 4.3 Conflict Resolution and Integration tool

No.	I am motivated by . . .	I am de-motivated by . . .
1		
2		
3		
4		
5		
6		
7		
8		
9		
10		
11		
12		
13		
14		
15		

Note: This table is available for download at www.performancecoachingtoolkit.com.

- What would help me to perform one step higher that I have up until now?

- When am I most productive? What's present in me at this time?

- When am I least productive? What's present in me at this time?

Study your lists in Table 4.2. Now consider the list of motivators there.

If you had all of the listed motivators in your job, what would still cause you to want to leave? Add anything that comes up for you in your 'de-motivator' column.

If you had all of the listed de-motivators in your job, what would still cause you to want to stay? Add anything that comes up for you in your 'motivator' column.

Can you remember a time when you were totally motivated? Take yourself back to that time right now. As you remember that specific time, as if you are there now, can you remember what happened just before you felt totally motivated? Record anything else that comes to mind in the 'motivator' column.

5 The Meta-programme Tool

Introduction

Meta-programmes come from the communication system called **neuro-linguistic programming** (NLP). These meta-programmes are a way of analysing and categorizing the way we and others psychologically process the world around us. They can be thought of as 'mental filters' with which we review and react to stimuli. It is important to remember that meta-programmes are 'temporary realities', in other words, they are a contrived way of looking at people, not the way people really are. In other words, our perceptions are 'our' reality but this is not the 'truth'. Despite this, they can be useful in supporting and influencing others. This tool provides a structure for analysing responses from a coachee and then formulating a response which 'talks their language' from the perspective of the meta-programme that they are using.

Learning outcomes

- Have a better understanding of how people around you think.
- Further understand your own motivators.
- Have strategies for understanding and influencing others.

Triggers

A sense that you are not connecting with the coachee or that their motivation is limited. For example, they may say:

- I'm not sure.
- Yeah, whatever.
- I'm not really interested in that.

Underpinning rationale

The more we can communicate in ways that match the thinking styles of others, the more rapport we will have. This engenders greater empathy and trust in the coachee. In addition, knowing what motivates others enables the coach to fine-tune the language they use in order to create motivational leverage in a conversation.

Instructions for use

Use the meta-programme recognition grid (Table 4.4) to familiarize yourself with the different meta-programmes. Begin to notice some of the trigger phrases as you listen to others or analyse your own speech patterns. Where appropriate and ethical, use the language patterns and approaches suggested in the last column of the recognition grid to match the meta-programmes of others.

TABLE 4.4 A set of useful meta-programmes

Meta-programme	Opposite	Type
Visual (Table 4.5)		Sensory
Auditory/Digital (Table 4.5)		Sensory
Kinaesthetic (Table 4.5)		Sensory
Towards (Table 4.6)	Away-from (Table 4.6)	
Judging (Table 4.7)	Perceiving (Table 4.7)	
Possibility (Table 4.8)	Necessity (Table 4.8)	
Matching (Table 4.9)	Mis-matching (Table 4.9)	

TABLE 4.5 A set of sensory meta-programmes

Sensory preference	Recognize by	Motivate by
Visual – process of information as pictures	May exhibit upward eye movements. Copious gesturing and language of pictures, e.g. 'I see what you mean'; 'that's a bright idea'; 'he's a colourful character'	Using visual language, e.g. 'Do you see what I mean?' 'Do you get the picture?'
Auditory – process information as sound and may externalize thought via talking through things with other people	May exhibit side-to-side eye movements. Little gesturing, and lots of auditory language, e.g. 'It sounds good in principle'; 'You're going to have to bang on at me, to get me to remember'	Using auditory responses, e.g. 'You seem in tune with that'; 'Who says you won't be able to hear the mood?'
Kinaesthetic – process via physical awareness and movement	May exhibit eye movements down and to the right. Slower processing with shifts of emotion. Language reflects sensation, e.g. 'This feels like a heavy topic to discuss'	Reflecting back their emotional and physical world, e.g. 'So you feel you have strong grip on next week's schedule now?' Build movement into coaching Using perceptual positions, resourceful space, sensory journeys, etc.
Auditory – process information in their head via self-talk	May exhibit eye movements down and to the left. What is said is often well constructed using technical and descriptive words, e.g. 'I sense this will satisfy the specification adequately'	Matching language by using more technical and descriptive terms and use Reflective Language, e.g. 'What is your analysis of this situation?'; 'What do you perceive to be the next specific action?'

TABLE 4.6 Towards and away-from meta-programmes

Preference	Recognize by	Motivate by
Towards	They may talk about what they want in the future, and positively stated	Aspirational, future target-setting, e.g. 'What would you like to have happen?', 'What if you could?'
Away-from	They may talk about what they do not want or wish to avoid. May use language including a desire to 'not have' something happen	Helping them identify negative consequences first. Then develop aspirational targets to help move them towards positive consequences

TABLE 4.7 Judging and perceiving meta-programmes

Preference	Recognize by	Motivate by
Judging	They often search for a 'right' answer, they believe that there is always a right and wrong way to do things	Giving them evidence, backing claims with research, acknowledging there is a wrong way to do things. Give precise instructions for a task and provide definitive answers
Perceiving	Happy to go with the flow and will believe that there are shades of grey in everything and will be happy to explore ideas without a defined purpose	Providing choices, allow periods of low pressure and time to make decisions. Avoid competitive activities

TABLE 4.8 Possibility and necessity meta-programmes

Preference	Recognize by	Motivate by
Possibility	They may use words like 'could', 'might', 'should', 'maybe', 'perhaps'. Voice may be relaxed	Using 'what if? questions, provide choice and speculative tasks
Necessity	Have a sense of duty and may use words 'like', 'must' and 'have to'. Compelled, imperative and may be critical. Voice can have an anxious or direct tone in it	Matching the language of necessity, e.g. 'you must', 'it is vital', 'this is really important'

TABLE 4.9 Matching and mis-matching meta-programmes

Preference	Recognize by	Motivate by
Matching	Easy agreement, even if you present an opposing view from one you put a few minutes before. Following your lead and body language	Behaving normally as they will follow any suggestions
Mis-matcher	Ritually and consistently disagrees with others. Body language constantly mis-matched. You may feel they are antagonistic	Offering the opposite view to the one you want them to consider. Use phrases like, 'You might not agree with me, but you might need to consider this question . . .?' This can cause them to agree with you in order to mis-match – you get your point across. Mirror body language but let them lead when you put your point across in the opposing format

Where do you go from here?

Once you have the main meta-programmes in your mind, you can begin to profile people you meet and then work out the main patterns of thinking they use – this knowledge can help you to quickly build rapport with them.

We have included here some of the main meta-programmes. There are many more one could add to these, to further sophisticate your usage of them. Reading further can assist your development in this area, for example, Sue Knight (2002: 35).

Within the tool

Build up a profile of the different meta-programme preferences a person is using. Bear in mind these may be context-dependent. For example, a co-worker who is not particularly happy in her job may use different meta-programme preferences in describing her job compared to her weekend mountaineering trip to the hills with her climbing partner.

Using other tools

Use the Tool T1 Well-formed Outcome and Tools T2 and T3 Visioning to build vision, targets and outcomes. Incorporate the language of the appropriate meta-programmes you have discovered from this tool in order to ratchet up the motivation levels of these future targets. Reflective Language helps to develop listening skills and the use of silence for sustaining self-reflection in the coachee is useful, see Tool CT1 The Principal Instruments of Coaching. Being present with the coachee is more important than thinking.

Further reading

Best, B. and Thomas, W. (2008) *Creative Teaching and Learning Resource Book*. London: Continuum International Publishing Group.

Dilts, R. (1990) *Changing Beliefs with NLP*. Capitola, CA: Meta Publications.

James, T. and Woodsmall, W. (1988) *Timeline Therapy and the Basis of Personality*. Capitola, CA: Meta Publications.

Thomas, W. and Smith, A. (2004) *Coaching Solutions, Practical Ways to Improve Performance in Education*. Stafford: Network Educational Press.

CHAPTER 5

Target Focus in STEPPPA

T 1 Well-formed Outcome

Introduction

Like **SMART goals**, Well-formed Outcome provide a framework for making sure that targets are significant, measurable, achievable, realistic and time-bounded.

Learning outcomes

Understand the importance of using a thorough model for setting targets.

Triggers

● Okay, I have a target, explored options and now have a preference for how to get there, what next?

Underpinning rationale

Highly successful people invariably have targets that have been considered carefully. These considerations will include: process, time-scales, personal impact, as well as the wider context. Targets that are researched thoroughly are less likely to be negatively influenced by surprises along the journey! The coachee will, consequently, tend to be more successful in achieving their target. We use an acrostic, PEAK STATE, to assist you in remembering the factors required for a well-formed outcome.

Instructions for use

A viable target will need to have certain important features. These are listed below. We have organized these features into an acrostic to aid its use and help memorize the content. The acrostic appears in a format that can be copied or downloaded (and then kept in a notebook or displayed on the wall). Use the PEAK STATE checklist (Table 5.1) to audit a target, to ensure it will have the maximum chance of success. Record as much as possible in a written form, as it is elicited from the coachee.

TABLE 5.1 The Well-formed Outcome checklist

Check Event	Advice
Present tense	Single target, stated in the present tense, e.g. I have . . ., I am . . ., I experience . . .
Experience	Coachee moves towards an emotional experience of what achieving the target would be like, 'Go into the future to a time in the future when you already have this X, what are you experiencing now that you have this X?'
Active emotionally	The coach can see the emotional association with the desired outcome in the coachee's physiology. The coach notices shifts in body clues (Tools CTS).
Key steps	The key steps towards the target are defined. For example, 'First, I will . . ., second, I will . . ., then I will . . ., and finally I will . . .
Sequential	There is a logical sequence to the key steps. Check these out with the coachee once the steps are established.
TTime-framed	There is a realistic time-frame to the key steps. Check this with questions like, 'In the context of everything else you have to do, how realistic is it for you to achieve X by time Y?'
Absolute and **A**uthority	The key steps are on a critical path with absolute certainty, in other words, no options left among the steps. The coachee also has the authority to carry out the steps. Check this out both by asking questions about the authority the coachee has, and also checking for authenticity with body clues.
Training	The coachee has the necessary expertise and skill to carry out the steps, or there are measures in place to ensure they gain this expertise (or have access to others who do). Check out that the coachee knows how to do the steps decided and question them about any gaps in their knowledge (and who might help them assess this objectively).
Energy and **E**ffects	The coachee has the energy in the form of 'will', to carry out the actions necessary. The effects of third party actions and attitudes on the steps are explored and any objections, conflicts or negative effects are anticipated. Questions such as, 'What, if anything, might prevent you from carrying this plan out? What will you do to counter the effects of any such issue?'

Key features of a Well-formed Outcome

- What is the single target?

- Has the coachee had an experience of what achieving that target is like?

- Are they physiologically energized when thinking/speaking about their target?

- What are the steps to the target?

- Are all steps time-framed, realistic and sequential?

- Are the steps sequential and free from any option?

- Check that the coachee has the authority, expertise and the will to achieve all individual steps themselves.

- Check that the coachee understands the energy, time and commitment required and has the energy, time and emotional resources to achieve the target.

- Check that the coachee understands third-party consequences and has realistically explored those as well as any likely objections, conflicting demands and negative effects (on important relationships with others).

- Check that they are ready to start the first step.

Where do you go from here?

Within the tool

Consider using other media that may appeal to the coachee in order to help them explore the process. These could include using charts, labels and pens rather than using question and answer alone.

Using other tools

Consider asking the coachee what they have learned and what they can now apply to other challenges and targets ahead of them.

2 The Vision-maker State

Introduction

A vision is a desired future. Although the word suggests it being a visual representation, it can also include what people will hear and say to themselves and what they will feel, taste and smell when they have achieved that desired state. This is a tool for clearing the mind and opening up the mind to creative thinking. If all this sounds a bit whacky, then let's bring it down to earth by providing an example from ordinary life. The experiences of our everyday lives put great expectations on our minds and overload us. When we are future planning, for example, it can take time for your head to stop spinning as if you have been on a roundabout for too long – your mind needs to slow down. To tap into your creative processes, it is necessary to 'still' the mind. Unless we practise this occasionally, we can easily forget how to relax and slow down. Ask yourself, how long does it take me to really relax when I go on holiday? This activity can help achieve a creative state quickly!

Learning outcomes

This tool will do the following:

- Calm down any internal psychological interference.
- Switch off unhelpful **internal dialogue**.
- Temporarily (or in some cases permanently) remove unhelpful feelings or beliefs about self or environment.
- Heighten creativity, intuition and clarity.

Triggers

When coachees are finding it difficult to be creative in their thinking, or when they are anxious about developing a positive future vision.

Underpinning rationale

For successful vision-development, it is vital that the mind is relaxed and alert. A jumble of self-talk and conflicting feelings in the coachee can prevent them from productive, creative thought.

Using the activities outlined here can help reduce both unhelpful self-talk and emotional interference.

Instructions for use

The Vision-maker state is created when your mind is calmed. For the vast majority of many people in their everyday lives, this calm state of being is a rarity. With practice, using the techniques outlined here, you can help calm the mind of the coachee so that they are prepared for creative activity.

- Find a peaceful place and either sit or stand in a comfortable position. Some people find bare feet comfortable and it is good to place these firmly on the floor.
- Close your eyes and imagine a circle of light around you. It might begin on the floor and then rise and envelop you in a warm and comfortable way.
- Next, become aware of all the thoughts and feelings that are not helpful to you in relaxing and in being creative. These might include feelings of pressure, anxiety, unhelpful 'self-talk' or limiting thoughts about your ability to be creative. Locate all of these unhelpful elements within yourself.
- Now, ask each of these unhelpful elements to leave you and to pass into the circle of light around you. They can remain there or even move outside the circle altogether. These unhelpful elements can come back in, if you still want them to, after the task is complete, but for now they are best left outside.
- Remain still until you have removed all of the unhelpful feelings and thoughts. Allow your mind to be still.
- Continue this for one to five minutes until you sense that there is quiet in your mind. During this time, if any thoughts enter your head, allow them to move out into the light that is around you.

The timing to achieve this can vary greatly depending on your previous experience. With practice, it is possible to calm the mind very rapidly using this approach. Equally, some people find that extending the period of focus heightens their creativity and clarity. We advise starting off for short periods (perhaps a few minutes only) in order to begin to notice the benefits. You can then lengthen the timing to suit yourself. People of all ages can be taught to do this. It is a brilliant technique for calming exam nerves and achieving a relaxed, alert state of mind for many reasons. These can include sport, presentations and dangerous situations that may require careful, uncluttered judgements. It is a superb way of developing both self-awareness and emotional intelligence. It can be used for anger-management and as a prelude to self-reflective work.

Some tips that help

- Create a circle around yourself with rope or cord to create a tangible zone into which to drop your 'intangible' feelings and thoughts.
- Be prepared to let go of negative emotions and thoughts, temporarily, if not permanently.

- There will often be distractions in the room, especially if this is done in groups; if leading the group, utilize the distractions, e.g., 'Hearing the sounds of cars going by only serves to deepen your clarity and stillness.'
- This also works really well for attacks of the giggles! For example, 'And giggling also helps you to further relax and empty your mind – every giggle helps you to release unhelpful thoughts and feelings.' You can say this in a very matter of fact way to yourself or a group – there is no need to sound like a psychiatrist!

Where do you go from here?

Within the tool

You can extend this activity by changing the length of time provided. It is a perfect precursor to any creative or analytical task. Use it before, during and after a psychologically taxing task, like report-writing, as it can energize you.

If you want to take this to a further stage, it is useful to carry out this task of clearing and then have a focus on resolving a particular challenge. It is best to find the challenge and also put it into the circle of light. Then, imagine a channel growing between the calm inner mind and the challenge outside. In your calm inner mind, find a source of energy for problem-solving (it can come from a past successful experience of solving a problem) and then allow this energy to flow through the channel into the challenge. Notice what it brings. If the coachee finds the idea of circles of light altogether weird, then having them simply move the thoughts and feelings outside themselves can be as helpful.

Using other tools

Try using Tool E3 Associated and Dissociated States and Tool E4 Anchoring to keep calm and focused. For other examples, see Best and Thomas (2008: 45).

3 Vision-builder – Four Tools in One

Introduction

This is a highly creative tool which forms the second of four steps of a comprehensive vision-building programme. It helps you to build a challenging vision and make it both realistic and manageable at the same time. A high quality vision for the future should be a challenge and be inspirational to achieve. In this tool you go through four phases:

1   Create the visioning state which prepares your mind (this is described in Tool T2 the Vision-maker State).

2   Generate ideas, create the future representation you want.

3   Define control and influence, which supports you to understand what you can action.

4   Embed the vision, turn your vision into goals. You embed the vision both consciously and unconsciously. The hidden or unconscious part of our mind is tremendously powerful in dictating our drives and motivations for everything we do in work and home life. This exercise engages you both at a conscious and unconscious level, making the end result more integrated, compelling and durable. It's subtle, but you can notice the difference!

Learning outcomes

By using this tool you will do the following:

●   Be in a creative state of mind for developing a vision.
●   Generate a range of effective and inspiring ideas.
●   Be clear about what you can influence in terms of control, in relation to your vision and what you have no control over.
●   Plant your vision firmly in your mind and formulate the words to confidently tell others about the vision.

Triggers

Any situation where a wider long-term vision is needed. It can be used organizationally, in teams and with individuals where they are asking a question like, 'What kind of future do we want to create?'

Instructions for use

For this activity (Best and Thomas 2008: 48), you will need the following resources: a quiet location, sticky notes or pieces of paper, three sheets of A4 paper and a pen.

Stage 1: The Visioning State

Use the steps in the previous tool to take yourself and your team/group into an appropriate state of mind for developing a vision. There is no point starting to create vision when you have limiting thoughts or feelings within you as this will interrupt the flow of creativity. This step reduces the impact of unhelpful internal dialogue and emotions.

Stage 2: Generating ideas

Once you have achieved the psychological 'stillness' from stage 1, you can then progress to stage 2.

- Give yourself permission to suspend judgement in this activity and adopt the idea that everything and anything is possible. No idea is too far-fetched.
- Imagine a future where everything is happening as you would like it in your workplace. It can be helpful to put a timescale on it, e.g. three years from now. What is happening? Consider:
  - What is happening in this future?
  - What am I seeing?
  - What am I hearing?
  - What am I feeling?
- Now write down all of the things you imagined happening in that future, putting each idea onto a separate piece of paper or a sticky note. Let your mind run with ideas and write them all down. Keep writing until you run out of ideas. Pause and wait for some more to come. They usually do! In a group, everyone does this.

Stage 3: Defining control and influence

This stage is useful in challenging our notions of what is, and what is not possible. Invariably, in this activity, we discover that very little is outwith our ability to control, and much is under direct control or influence. It is a tremendously energizing and inspiring group activity.

- Set out an imaginary line on the floor and take three pieces of A4 paper and on one write the word 'Control', on another the word 'Influence' and another, the words 'No control'. Lay out the cards on the floor, (Figure 5.1).
- Now, go and stand on the floor with all of your sticky note ideas in your hand. Then walk forward 'into the future' and take one idea at a time and consider, is it something you have control over, something you can influence or something you have no control over? Place the idea in the appropriate zone on the floor 'in the future'. Now, repeat this until you have set down all of your ideas.

- Once you have all your ideas in place, start to consider for each idea: those you can control or influence and how, along a 'timeline', they can be accomplished. Move the sticky notes, still in line with the labelled cards, to a position along the timeline where you feel they could be accomplished
- Prioritize them.

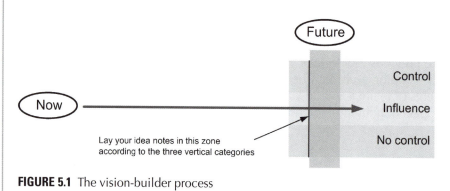

FIGURE 5.1 The vision-builder process

Stage 4: Embed the vision

- Now, go and stand by each vision-outcome and close you eyes to think about each one in turn. Once again, imagine the ring of light around you and move any unhelpful thoughts or feelings out of yourself. Now, imagine you have already achieved this outcome again. What are you feeling? What are you seeing? What are you hearing now that you have achieved this? Importantly, ask yourself to bring to mind the final thing that will happen to let you know that you have achieved this outcome.
- Then, make sure you are facing the future on the timeline and, standing next to the first of your prioritized outcomes, imagine once more that the outcome is achieved. Bring to mind the final event that will happen (to let you know that you have achieved the outcome) and then take three deep breaths in and out – with each out-breath imagine breathing energy into the outcome. Then open your eyes. Do this for each priority outcome.
- The last part of the process is to stand back at NOW and with your eyes closed, imagine drawing the timeline in your mind. Imagine the timeline becoming integrated inside you with all of the outcomes laid out accomplished in the future. Take three more deep breaths in and out, and you are finished. You will now find it easy to articulate your vision to others with energy and enthusiasm because you have effectively lived the end-result through this process and will have created a memory of the successful outcome in the future.

What often happens during this process is, a gentle psychological play between the act of 'experiencing' a real outcome and 'knowing' that you have not! The conflict between these two is not uncomfortable, just interesting. As you let the logical mind slow down, so the experiencing of this new and pleasant psychological state becomes more real and complete. This experiencing 'as if real' helps to harness the subconscious mind to your vision and will. Conventional goal-setting techniques impose a highly logical, 'How will I achieve this outcome?'. Such approaches are limiting in their motivation – when you harness the whole mind, not just what is logical, your chance of success is much greater.

Where do you go from here?

Within the tool

We strongly recommend that you don't create a rigid action plan to go with your vision! We know this may surprise you, but there is a growing body of research which suggests that outcomes are best achieved through creating a cognitive dissonance between what your sub-conscious mind believes to be true, and what is logically true. In other words, if you create a representation in your mind of the end-point of your vision (and the stepped successes along the route), this conditions your subconscious to look creatively for opportunities to have this outcome achieved.

Using other tools

This tool is complemented by Tool PL1 Logical Wheels, Tool PL2 Time Trail and Tool PA3 Letting Go.

T

4 A Future in Art

A pictorial means of expression can help some coachees to experience and express their hopes and aspirations for the future. An artistic approach, however rudimentary, can be a very effective way of generating targets and for exploring hidden beliefs, whether limiting or aspirational.

Learning outcomes

- Uncover the hidden metaphors and beliefs early in a coaching assignment.
- Enable coachees to express themselves in non-verbal ways.

Triggers

Any situation where it is helpful for a coachee to think about their aspirations and their targets:

- I want to get on and make the future happen.
- I am not very good with words.
- I am not sure what the future holds.

Underpinning rationale

For some coachees, drawing or creating a doodle of their current situation and of their future is easier than trying to put these into words. This technique works especially well with younger coachees and with people who are not used to expressing themselves openly in front of others. The stimulus of a drawing enables an easy and free dialogue revealing much about their aspirations, but also about their assumed limits and other **psychological construct**s. This information can be helpful to the coachee in achieving their goals. It can be a great rapport-builder, sometimes with humour emerging from it.

Instructions for use

Resources

Sheets of paper in A2, A3 and A4 sizes, coloured pens, pencils. Introduce the idea of drawing or doodling in a low-risk way. Here are examples:

> One way that people find it helpful to think about the things they want in the future, is to draw it. Rather than the word, draw, you may prefer doodle or scribble – whatever works for you. This exercise is all to do with expression and not about art. Whatever you put on paper is perfect for the purpose of expression.

> If you will, I wonder if you would like to divide this sheet of paper in half and on one half represent yourself as you see yourself now and on the other half of the paper represent yourself as you see yourself in your desired future. Take all the time need. You may like to show things literally as you see them, or you might like to use some kind of metaphor or analogy, it's up to you.

Once their expression is complete, without judgement, proceed to ask the coachee to talk you through the representations they have drawn. Use curious questioning to tease out desires, fears, limits, motivations, expectations, etc. If the representation is literal, then use questioning which is literal and if it is metaphorical, use questioning which encourages exploration within the metaphor, for example, 'So, what does that star represent for you? What is it like being that star?'

Where do you go from here?

Within the tool

Support the development of understanding with Exquisite Listening, Reflective Language and Clean Language questioning. Pay attention to macro- and micro-differences in the 'now' and 'future' images. For example, if they draw themselves smaller in the future, compared to now, ask them about that, 'I notice that you are smaller here than there. What is that about?'

Using other tools

Use Tool T2 the Vision-maker State and Tool T1 Well-formed Outcome to encourage greater context. Use this to encourage a honed, single, workable target.

5 The Goal Summary Tool

Introduction

A simple template for collecting and recording goals from Tool S3 the Wheel of Work.

Learning outcomes

It is important for the coachee to keep a record of goals in order to refer back to them. The coach also needs to have the same record to keep the coachee accountable for achieving those goals.

Triggers

For example, use after Tool S3 the Wheel of Work.

Underpinning rationale

Goals which are written down and recorded in accordance with Tool T1 the Well-formed Outcome are more likely to be achieved. In addition, it is useful to the coachee to be able to track their own progress toward the goals.

Instructions for use

Use Table 5.2 to record goals.

TABLE 5.2 Goal summary

Name	Date		
Goal Area	*Goal*	*Well-formed Outcome*	*Prompt*
Job satisfaction	**P**resent tense		
Learning and development	**E**xperience		
Reward and recognition	**A**ctive emotionally		
Purpose and passions	**K**ey steps		

Change	**S**equential
Work–life balance	**T**ime-framed
Career progression	**A**bsolute and Authority
Relationships	**T**raining
	Energy and Effects

Where do you go from here?

Within the tool

Use the Well-formed Outcome prompt in Table 5.2 to guide the formation of goals. Refer to Tool T1 the Well-formed Outcome tool for further information.

Using other tools

Use STEPPPA to enhance emotional drive to the targets, creating any necessary perceptual shifts and to generate actions towards the targets.

6 Locus of Control

Introduction

'Locus of control' (LOC) is a neat way to describe where we place responsibility for what happens to us in our lives. The concept of LOC can be used to assist a coachee to acknowledge psychological blind spots (scotomas) and to take more responsibility for a situation. This will help them to reach their goals.

Learning outcomes

LOC is a useful way for anyone to consider the degree to which they are taking control of their destiny. In different situations people need to take more or less responsibility for what is happening to them.

Triggers

First, not enough responsibility is being taken, perhaps signified by statements like these:

- She's always blocking me.
- It's not my week.
- They always get in the way.

Second, over-responsibility is being taken:

- I am trying so hard to make things right between the two of them and they won't listen to me.
- There's just too much to do and I am sinking.

Underpinning rationale

In some situations coachees blame others, organizations and nameless entities. Invariably, their complaints are justification when they are *not* achieving their goals. This blaming of others diminishes the individual's power; they are letting go of their control; they may feel helpless. In extremis, it can lead to symptoms of depression. In other situations, coachees can take on so much responsibility that they feel that everything and everyone around them is their responsibility, so-called neurosis. This can overwhelm them and lead to a paralysis of action. By assisting coachees to consider a continuum of responsibility, they can gain a more objective view on their situation.

Instructions for use

This tool can either be done sitting down or, for a much more engaging and powerful experience, it can be mapped on the floor using labels. The labels can be connected with lines formed with chalk or rope. We give here the floor-based version of the tool, which you may adapt to a more sedentary version (Figure 5.2).

Use chalk, string or rope to connect across the room and set down two labels, 'External Locus of Control' (E-LOC) and 'Internal Locus of Control' (I-LOC). Similarly, taking a sheet of paper, draw a line across page with I-LOC at one end and E-LOC at the other end.

First, stand at the E-LOC with your coachee and explain. For example, say something like, 'The external locus of control is where we put the responsibility for what's happening to us outside of ourselves. We lay that responsibility on other people, organizations or things happening around us. So we might blame the weather, the time of year, the prime minister, a friend, our genes or some other factor beyond our control.'

Then, stand at the other end of the line with your coachee and explain, 'The internal locus of control is where we take responsibility inside of ourselves and decide our goals, our pathway to those goals and how we will get there. If things get in the way of achieving our goals, then we adapt to overcome the difficulties. If we cannot adapt, then we come to accept that which we cannot control – we adapt our goals accordingly. On occasion we can take so much responsibility that we can become overwhelmed by what we feel responsible for, for example, other people's feelings, other people's jobs and the wider issues in the world. Making progress is often about finding a balance between how much responsibility to take and how much to let go.'

Then you can ask your coachee some or all of the following questions:

- In your life, in general, where on this line do you spend your time?
- Are there any particular times, or situations, during which you spend more time at one end of the line than the other?
- What are you learning about yourself as you explore this line?
- Are there troubling aspects of this line and are there rewarding aspects of this line too?
- What emotions and instincts does this stimulate in you?

Now, ask your coachee to establish where the 'present time' can be represented on the floor and invite them to go there (if they move, go with them). Ask the coachee to establish where

FIGURE 5.2 Locus of control

the future is in relation to that space and to look there. Then ask them to locate where the 'past' is and invite them to look there. Ask them, 'Where have you spent most of your time in the past in relation to <the key issue they want to focus on>? Would you like to move there?' Facilitate them to enhance their experience of that past.

Now ask them to move towards the future space (with a real sense of journeying into the future) and to stand where they would like to be in the future in relation to their LOC. Ask them, 'So, here we are, what are you experiencing in this time, what do you feel, see and hear?' You will assist them if you use the present tense (see Tool CT8 Tenses). For example, 'So, what are you feeling right now?' and, 'What is this doing for you, now that you have it?'

After this, ask your coachee to turn around and look back at the journey they have taken to reach this point. Ask them, 'In order to arrive here and have what you have now, what did you do and what decisions did you make to get here?' 'What did you do differently back then, that enabled you to change and make this happen?'

Record each action and decision on a footprints template (Figure 5.3) and lay these on the floor, in sequential order. Once they have reviewed and corrected if necessary, ask them to walk the sequence from the present to the future and check again that it makes sense to them. They may wish to add further steps or even simplify their path. Then gather up the footsteps in order and number them. Give them to the coachee.

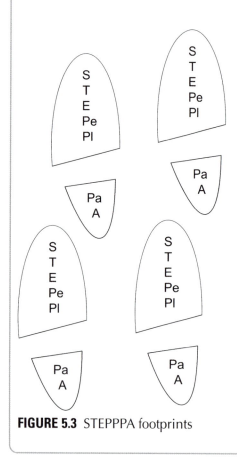

FIGURE 5.3 STEPPPA footprints

Where do you go from here?

Within the tool

Use the tool as a reference point and ask the coachee throughout coaching to consider how they are thinking about an issue in relation to the LOC. These reflections can help shift the coachee's perception. If you both keep a notational record of where the coachee senses they are on the line, then it can also provide a semi-quantitative measure of progress for review later.

Using other tools

The full LOC will lead to any number of STEPPPA tools. To wrap up, use the Tool PA4 Taking Learning Forward.

Further reading

Best, B. and Thomas, W. (2008) *Creative Teaching and Learning Resource Book*. London: Continuum International Publishing Group.

McDermott, I. and Jago, W. (2003) *The NLP Coach*. London: Piatkus.

McLeod, A. (2003) *Performance Coaching: The Handbook for Managers, HR Professionals and Coaches*. Carmarthen and New York: Crown House Publishing.

CHAPTER 6

Emotional Focus in STEPPPA

E 1 Making it Personal

Introduction

This tool represents a means to help a coachee have greater emotional association with their experience. More authentic and meaningful dialogue results from this and then change becomes easier to facilitate.

Learning outcomes

Understand why, when and how to encourage greater psychological association with their emotional experience.

Triggers

The coachee may say:

● You are uncomfortable in that situation.
● One is unhappy when that happens.
● You just feel angry.

Underpinning rationale

When the coachee is describing their own experience they may use the words 'you' and 'one' instead of the personal pronoun 'I'. This *can* indicate a lack of attachment or 'psychological association' with their experience. When a coachee needs to experience more motivation (or de-motivation), it can be helpful to encourage more psychological association with their emotional experience, for example, by asking them to consider making it personal to them.

Instructions for use

When you wish a coachee to be more emotionally connected to an experience, use two questions to encourage this increased emotional connectivity. Ask them:

● Do you mean that 'you' are uncomfortable in that situation?
● Do you mind repeating that you are uncomfortable, but using the word 'I' instead of 'one'?

Where do you go from here?

Within the tool

Watch for physiological changes that could indicate a higher 'association' with their experience and leave any productive silence to run after they have spoken. The changes you notice might include:

● change in skin tones (more pale or more red);
● change in breathing (slow or faster);
● change in muscle tones (slouching or stiffer);
● more dramatic changes including crying.

If they say the phrase quickly without a pause, and without changes in their physiology, ask them to repeat it again, but more deliberately and slowly. If there are signs of change in them, ask them once again or consider using the same phrase yourself, very accurately in composition, pace and tone but perhaps a little more quietly.

Using other tools

Greater association with experiences provides motivation or de-motivation, both of which can be helpful to their outcome. If the coachee has not done any work with you in revisiting past situations (as if they are happening in that moment), Sensory Journeys (or other imagined and experienced situations that might arise in the future), now might be a good time to explore further emotional stretching. Perhaps provide similar exercises as homework.

Use Time Trail (p. 138), Tool PL2 or Tool E3 Associated and Dissociated States.

2 Naming Emotions

Introduction

When a coachee is talking about a significant experience, then the ability to name any associated emotions can be an important first step to making a change in that experience. Adding language to feelings helps to bring them at least two things: the first to be more in touch, or psychologically associated, with their experience, and, second, to add greater conscious awareness to their experience. This cognitive awareness can make change easier to achieve. Greater emotional depth can help them to motivate themselves.

Learning outcomes

- Recognition of the two extremes of emotional intelligence.
- When and how to encourage greater emotional experience.
- When and how to facilitate less emotional experience.

Triggers

The coachee is experiencing, or has experienced, something important emotionally but they are vague about what the specific emotions behind that are.

Underpinning rationale

People experience the world emotionally but are not always able to identify those emotions. Once an emotion is named, one can focus on enhancing or attenuating that emotion, if desired. The science of emotional intelligence suggests that self-awareness of emotional states is critical to personal change and also to making faster progress in both the understanding and managing of other people. Naming emotions is a good first step on that developmental journey.

Instructions for use

Typical statements the coach may use include:

- So, when she says something like that and you have this experience of 'tense', what else is there about 'tense' and does that have a name?
- Well, some people might experience irritability, like maybe wanting to get back at them, or having lots of unproductive internal dialogue, or wanting to get away and do and experience something away from that. And others might be angry and may want to shout or hit out if they could, and their hearts may be beating harder. I'm not saying you should have any of those experiences when she says that to you, but if there is something else, what is that something else that you experience as she says that to you now?

Where do you go from here?

Within the tool

Even if a coachee cannot name their emotion, any indication of something experienced (and associated with their experience) can act as a place to start experimenting with. The coach may ask:

- So, what would I have to do to experience that?
- And what does it take to have more (or less) of that?

And keep pushing for the development of such awareness in other aspects of their coaching experience.

If they have been very associated with the emotional state and it is not helpful to them, remember to think about asking them to move to a more resourceful place in the room (see Tool AT2 Resourceful Spaces). 'If there was somewhere else in the room where you can be more resourceful, where is that resourceful place in the room and can you go there?'

Using other tools

Awareness and management of the coachee's association with their material are a significant adjunct to this tool, see Tool E3 Associated and Dissociated States. Where the coachee is already experiencing their emotional world and able to express it, a wider range of tools may be used. Where the coachee is less able, consider frequent use of Tool PA1 the Ranking Question so you both get a measure of their motivation, the extent of their experience and of their commitment. The coach's awareness of coachee state is helped by advanced ability in Tool CT5 Body Clues.

3 Associated and Dissociated States

Introduction

Emotional attachment to an experience can enrich that experience and provide the coachee with motivating (or de-motivating) feelings that are powerful precursors for coached change. Emotional attachment is not always helpful or useful. The coach needs to be able to notice, understand and manage emotional states by facilitation.

Learning outcomes

- Know how to notice associated and dissociated psychological states.
- Know how to enrich states or create detachment from states.

Triggers

- The coachee is stuck in a demanding situation but describes their situation matter-of-factly without particular expression.
- The coachee is very upset about a situation and finds it difficult to be logical about it.

Underpinning rationale

Emotions are at the core of our motivation and de-motivation whether expressed in words or not. The coachee may not be able to understand or explain their emotional experiences in any coherent way but their emotions are still at the heart of their motivation or de-motivation.

Instructions for use

The coachee may be 'matter-of-fact' in what may be difficult circumstances. The following language patterns are useful for the coach as they help the coachee to associate into their emotions:

General move to associated state

'If there was something physical or a feeling you noticed when you talk about that experience, what is that physical difference or feeling?'

Referencing the experience of others

'So you are here, and the situation is happening now. Other people might experience tension, aches, or sleep poorly after situations like this. I am not saying you should have any of those experiences, but I wonder if there is something that you experience now?'

Trigger language – make it more real

'So, I'm your boss, say, and I am going to use that same phrase again, just like that <says phrase> so what is it like to hear that now?' The coach needs to watch for reactions to the accurate use of the phrase.

Raising internal awareness

'What else do you notice about your experience, is there more internal dialogue or discomfort, for example?'

Dissociating from an emotional state

If the coachee is unable to be logical because of the emotional association with the issue: 'Imagine there is somewhere else in this room where it is more relaxed (for you) to be, where is that and could you go there now?'

The technique is adapted from Tool AT2 Resourceful Spaces. 'Let's think where we are now, in this room. I'm sitting here with this blue shirt on and there are, how many windows and chairs are there in here?'

The coach is trying to get logical, thinking processes going. These occur in the upper brain, or cerebrum, rather than in the mid-brain, where much emotional activity takes place.

Visual pattern alternative

If they seem to be quite visually developed, you could say: 'If you will, imagine in your mind that you can see both of you in that place, like a picture, and if you will, put that picture further away from you and as you do so, make it more remote from you, be more detached and just observe what is really happening with them.'

Where do you go from here?

Within the tool

Where intense psychological states are being experienced, particularly unhelpful states, remember to help break their state afterwards by bringing their attention back to the room and yourself – use gestures and language to get their full attention and help them use cognition. Think about asking them to move to a different and more useful place in the room (as illustrated above).

Using other tools

Look out for the use of the words 'you' or 'one' when the coachee is talking about their own experiences (see Tool E1 Making it Personal). Think about using Tool PA1 the Ranking Question to help them to calibrate their experiences. What else might they need to experience that is helpful to their learning and motivation? Ask them! Tool S1 the Pattern Breaker may also be useful. Other tools that exercise a coachee's ability to change state at will include Tool E4 Anchoring, Tool PL2 Time Trail, Tools PE7 and PE8 Perceptual Positions.

4 Anchoring

Introduction

Anchoring is a term coined by practitioners of neuro-linguistic programming (NLP) to describe a conditioning process whereby a stimulus and a behaviour are linked together by psychological association. For example, the clicking of a person's fingers at the same time as they naturally feel elated, will create an association between the finger clicking and the elated feeling. With sufficient emotional intensity and repetition of this association, the fingers may be clicked at a time (when an emotional state is less resourceful), and the feeling of elation will be triggered. This can then be very useful to the coachee in situations where they are feeling un-resourceful and when they would like to be able to trigger an instant improvement in their emotional state.

Learning outcomes

Know how to create an anchor to stimulate a **resourceful state** in a coachee.

Triggers

Anchors can be set up to change the coachee's future experiences of a recurring event that they dislike. Anchors can also be used when a coachee knows that they have to do something which they are fearful or anxious about. For example:

● irrational fear of a particular manager;
● an interview or presentation which they anticipate will be stressful;
● before exploring a potentially emotionally difficult topic in a coaching conversation.

Underpinning rationale

Anchors work because they are based upon the principle of Classical Conditioning of Carlson (1986: 506). A stimulus and a behaviour can become associated together. This happens in normal human existence, often without us noticing. A phrase of music or speech can invoke a powerful emotional response. When one sets up an anchor, one is simply creating a new stimulus that is associated with a more useful and resourceful psychological state or being.

A well-known set of experiments on the digestive functions of dogs was carried out by the Russian scientist, Ivan Pavlov in the 1890s.

Instructions for use

This is a template for installing an anchor for a coachee using a 'physical' anchor.

1   Ensure you have strong rapport with a coachee.

2   Explain the anchoring process to a coachee.

3   Explain that the process of anchoring will require that you touch them on the knuckle. Ask them if that is okay and get their permission.

4   Ask the coachee to recall a specific past event where they felt totally energized and ask them to 'go back to that event and experience it now and as you get that experience again, what do you feel, what do you see and what are you hearing now you are totally energized?'

5   Watch the coachee and as you see their physiology change in response to their thoughts and experiencing, judge when this physiology is developing and press them gently but firmly on a specific knuckle joint. Keep that pressure while their new state is *maintained or increasing* in its effect. If their state reverses, immediately release the pressure and remove your finger. Get the coachee to break their physiological state of mind by standing or moving in some way. Or ask them questions to make them focus elsewhere and to process that information.

6   Repeat this a few times. Notice that the ability of the coachee to change state will typically get faster and more extreme. It may take, typically, two to eight repeats to install the anchor and to notice the change in speed and effect, sometimes more. When you have a fast and powerful reaction, move to the next step – test the anchor!

7   Test the anchor by pressing the knuckle. If the anchor is strong, you will see the physiology shift as you saw previously, but in response to the touch alone! If they don't shift, repeat steps 1–6.

To create a really powerful, positive anchor, repeat stages 1–6 with each of the following peak experiences to enhance their experience:

● Laughing uproariously

● Feeling totally loved

● Completely confident

● Idyllically happy.

'Stack' the anchor onto the same knuckle for each of these to create a really powerful experience when triggered. Once you have successfully tested the anchor, explain to the coachee that they can now trigger this anchor for themselves in situations where they would like more resourceful feelings. Suggest that they use it several times each day in the first week, once a day in the week that follows and regularly after that, until the anchor is always predictable and powerful.

Where do you go from here?

Within the tool

Enhancements include the following:

- You think the coachee needs to really experience the feelings of the past experience. Talk your coachee into deep association into the state using phrases like, 'and just how good does that feel/look now that you are feeling/seeing that now?' and, 'have that feeling, sound or picture increase so it feels/looks/sounds the best it can be.'

- You sense that the coachee will benefit from having a very different set of feelings to the ones they currently have in particular circumstances. Go into that state of mind yourself (being really energized, confident, etc.), as you invite your coachee to do the same. This gives a physiological 'permission' for to them to access that same state themselves.

You can also ask the coachee to set the physical anchor themselves with a knuckle or other specific touch that they would never use accidently in normal life. You can ask the coachee to select a physical or other psychological representation to use as the anchor and work with that.

Using other tools

Anchoring is very useful when combined with Tool PL2 Time Trails. Other tools that help train the coach to 'manage' learning states in the coachee include Tools PE7 and PE8 Perceptual Positions and the coaching resource Neutrality and Exquisite Listening (p. 184).

5 Resolution of Inner Conflict

Introduction

Coachees may often bring examples of conflicts which they are running in their internal dialogue. These conflicts can prevent them from making progress and cause unresourceful feelings that then frustrate their best efforts.

Learning outcomes

Understand how to resolve conflict in internal dialogue.

Triggers

The coachee may say:

- Half of me wants to do this and the other doesn't.
- I feel torn between these options.
- Part of me is completely up for the change and the other is not.

Underpinning rationale

Internal conflict of this nature arises when a coachee's values and beliefs are at odds with one another. In order to successfully overcome the conflict and make empowered decisions, the coachee needs to find common ground between the two conflicting elements. This process externalizes the conflicting beliefs/values and allows the coachee to find out what each element has in common with the other. The result is a resolution between the two conflicting parts.

Instructions for use

1 Ensure you have good rapport with the coachee.

2 Invite the coachee to talk about the conflict and encourage them to separate out the two conflicting parts of their thinking.

3   Say, 'If you will, bring the part that is your desired response to your conflict out of yourself and have it sit on the table in front of you.'

4   Once the 'desired' part is there in front of them, ask, 'Does it remind you of anyone and does this part have a name?' Get the name from them and use it in referring to this part subsequently.

5   Next ask, 'What is the highest positive purpose that this part <use name of part> has for you?'

6   Whatever they announce, feed it into this question, 'and <name of highest positive purpose> is for what positive purpose?'

7   Repeat step six for each subsequent purpose given until the coachee can provide no further purpose or until their responses loops back to a previously stated purpose. Take the highest level purpose and state, 'So, it wants <highest positive purpose>.'

8   Say, 'Now turn your attention to the other part of you that. If you will, bring this part out somewhere else on the table. Does it remind you of anyone and does it have a name?' Get the name from them and use it in referring to this part subsequently.

9   Next, ask, 'What is the highest positive purpose that this part <use name of part> has for you?'

10   Whatever they announce, feed it into this question, 'and <name of part> is for what positive purpose?'

11   Repeat step 10 until the purpose for the second part is the same as that for the first part (which will happen!).

12   Once the purpose of the second part is the same as the first, respond with, 'So, <name of first part> and <name of second part> both want <insert common purpose>. What is happening to them now that they realize they both want the same thing?' Await response.

13   Once the coachee has responded, ask the following questions:
   (a)   'Now that they realize they want the same thing, what gifts might they offer one another?'
   (b)   'What is happening on the table now that they have exchanged gifts?'
   (c)   'Now that <names of parts> are reunited, I wonder if you will take them back inside to reintegrate with the whole of you now. Let me know when that is complete.'

Where do you go from here?

Within the tool

Occasionally people resist the reintegration of the parts. This can be countered by saying, 'I know that up until this point they had not wanted to come together, and I wonder now that they think about it, what they might need from one another that they can give freely right now, or both let go of, such that they can come together now, as one?'

A coach must always judge the receptivity of a coachee to a particular technique. This tool can be perceived by some coachees as being a little 'out of the box'. If you think the idea of bringing imaginary parts out onto the table and calling them after your mother is a bit spooky for your coachee, then modify the approach. One modification is to leave out the question about who it reminds you of and simply ask them to, 'hold each of these parts in their mind separately, for now' and work on them in that way. Another is simply to reflect the conflicting information and ask them how they manage to hold on to these two conflicting things at the same time. Yet another, is to ask them what you (the coach) would need to do and believe to hold onto, and live with, two opposing 'voices' at the same time. In their cognitive rationalization, they may discover both the will, and the way, to resolve their own conflict.

Another alternative is to for you to get the coachee to talk about their conflict and then invite them to use your own hands to represent the two opposing 'voices', for example, You say: 'So, I hear you say that there's a bit of you that wants to take the holiday and a bit that doesn't.' As you say this, hold your hands up and imagine and display as if each part is sitting on each hand. Now repeat steps 5–14. Substitute any words which might be inappropriate for the coachee, for example, instead of using the concept of mutual gifts, substitute the word 'gift' for 'advice'.

Finish the process by checking the outcome. Say, for example, 'I would like you now, if you will, to go out into the future, to a time when you that old situation comes up again, but you are aware now that it is different.' Repeat several times with different events in the future until you are confident the coachee is convinced things have changed for them.

Using other tools

Once the conflict is resolved, Tool T1 Well-formed Outcome can be created and Tool PL2 Time Trail can be employed to build a compelling future.

6 Affirmations

Introduction

Introduction

An affirmation is a positive phrase, description or sentence that outlines how you wish to behave, think or feel. Affirmations are particularly useful to support self-confidence and can act as mantras for people, so they can block negative self-talk during, for example, public-speaking. They will be based on goals that a person sets for themselves. Affirmations have several key components that we represent by the acronym, RPM.

Relevant to the coachee – make sure it supports a coachee-centred goal and is described in words that they feel comfortable with.

Positive and present – set the affirmations in terms of what *is* wanted rather than what *is not* wanted and, state in the present tense.

Moving and motivating – add movement to the affirmation and emotional content to inspire the coachee.

Learning outcomes

- Coachees come to learn that what they run as **script**s, in their heads, affects their performance both negatively and positively.
- Affirmations provide motivating and goal-focused self-talk to block negative self-talk and to encourage performance and belief-change.

Triggers

Coachees who:

- report negative self-talk that is interfering with their performance;
- significantly use negative language patterns such as, 'I am going to not be tired' which is reinforcing the tiredness rather stating something positive;
- need a mantra to focus on positive performance in the lead-up to, or during, performances such as interviews, presentations, stage shows, and so on.

Underpinning rationale

Affirmations block unhelpful self-talk and can re-write negative scripts (when the mantra is followed by success, in an area of endeavour). The language is carefully constructed using simple rules to ensure that the affirmation has a positive and supportive effect.

Instructions for use

Develop and write down affirmations that support the coachee's goal.

Make it RPM

Relevant to the coachee – make sure it supports a coachee-centred goal and is in words they feel comfortable with, for example, for improved confidence, 'I am confident in all that I do.'

Positive and present – set the affirmations in terms of what *is* wanted rather than what *is not* wanted and, state in the present tense, for example, 'I don't want to feel nervous when I speak to the board' is likely to reinforce nervousness, whereas 'I am calm and inspiring' reinforces the outcomes that the coachee wants to have.

Moving and motivating – add movement to the affirmation and emotional content to inspire the coachee, for example, 'I am being confident', or, 'I am responding positively to customer enquiries.'

Write your goal here

Affirmation doodles

Now, jot down a range of affirmations – use the RPM rules above, and then find an affirmation wording that totally works for you. Doodle if you want.

Now settle on the affirmation that works for you.

Where do you go from here?

Encourage your coachee to repeat their affirmation to themselves ten times in the morning and ten in the evening and to repeat the affirmation again at times when they are specifically engaging in the goal that they wrote it for.

Within the tool

Prompt and question coachees in order to encourage them to experiment with language and to get the affirmation just right for them. Get them to apply the RPM rules.

My affirmation

Using other tools

This tool is useful when used in conjunction with Tool S1 the Pattern Breaker. It can also usefully be combined with Tool AT6 Strengths Inventory adapted for use by the coachee and worked on as 'homework'.

7 SODs, Hot Words and Phrases

Introduction

Words that diminish ownership of plans and undermine self-management can be identified as triggers for intervention by the coach. These words are part of a 'hot' vocabulary and include 'should', 'ought' and 'duty' – the SODs. They can disempower coachees.

Learning outcomes

An awareness of 'HOT word' triggers for coaching intervention.

Triggers

SODs and others words, including 'must'. For example:

- I must do this by tomorrow.
- I have to go to the meeting.
- It's imperative that she agrees.
- I really ought to.
- It's essential that . . .
- It's my duty.
- I should go now.

Underpinning rationale

People often lack commitment, motivation and diminish their prospect of success if they feel they are forced to do something. If their mindset is like that of a victim, then they are unlikely to gain self-determination and self-respect from any single episode of their success. Challenging their language can lead to new perspectives and to a healthier mindset for success. These underpin self-determined achievement.

Instructions for use

Hot words in regard to self (even when spoken of in the second person, for example 'one should not break any confidence') include, 'should', 'ought', 'duty' and 'must'. A suitable challenge is for you to ask 'Should? Who says?'

A coach might be tempted to help the coachee explore a possible commitment to *not* doing something that is, say, dutiful. First, we recommend encouraging attention *towards* the ownership of the issue and whether there is a will to change that.

Where do you go from here?

Within the tool

Typically one might follow the challenge by asking about alternate courses of action (and inaction) and then questioning to help identify the best choice for them.

Using other tools

Sometimes the challenges lead to a deeper root cause in their past. In this case, questioning and seeking objective, pragmatic views about the earlier experiences can help transform the current mindset. Using Tool PE8 the Third Perceptual Position can help with that. Any new, healthy pattern of response to hot words can be underpinned by using Time Trails (p. 138). Where the hot words form part of an established pattern, Tool S1 the Pattern Breaker and Tool E4 Anchoring can help reinforce a new, healthier response.

As well as 'hot words', there are 'hot phrases', including any self-**limiting belief** and the phrase 'have to'. We provide a list of some of these words and phrases in Appendix 3.

Further reading

McLeod, A. (2003a) *Performance Coaching: The Handbook for Managers, HR Professionals and Coaches.* Carmarthen and New York: Crown House Publishing.
McLeod, A. (2003b) Emotion and coaching, *Anchor Point,* 17(2): 35–41.
Scott, S. (2002) *Fierce Conversations.* London: Piatkus Books.

PErception Focus in STEPPPA

PE

1 Objective Advice

Introduction

This tool encourages coachees to generate objective viewpoints about their situation. It does this by inviting them to consider how others would advise them, if they were to ask for an opinion.

Learning outcomes

- Coachees gain a series of alternative perspectives on a challenge, problem or dilemma.
- Coachees cast aside un-resourceful feelings in order to meet a challenge.

Triggers

Coachees making statements like:

- I am stuck.
- No idea what to do next.
- I am completely confused.
- I only have one option, and it's not ideal.

Underpinning rationale

When the coachee's emotions are proving counter-productive to their progress, objective advice can help to create a degree of dissociation from the emotional experience of their challenge. Alongside this, the tool also helps a person to take different perceptual positions and to see the issue differently.

Instructions for use

Follow the instructions in the tool template.

Using objective advice

Redefine the challenge you face and write it down in no more than 25 words.

Now that you have defined the challenge, consider the likely viewpoints of the following people. Record your thinking in Table 7.1. Remember this tool is not about actually asking these people, but about guessing what they would say to you.

TABLE 7.1 Authenticity tracker

Relation to you	Actual individual	Their objective advice
Someone you admire		
Someone you care about		
Someone who makes you laugh		
An animal		
Someone else who is or has been significant in your life		

Note: This table is downloadable at www.performancecoachingtoolkit.com.

Once you have recorded your thinking, consider, with your coach:

- What have I learned about your original perspective on this challenge?
- How has my view changed?
- What's next?

Where do you go from here?

Proceed onto the next stage in the STEPPPA model to conclude the coaching session.

Within the tool

The coach may keep an 'encouraging' tone throughout. If coachees are unwilling or unable to make the perceptual shift and respond by saying, 'I don't know', give them a second stab at it by responding, 'If you were to know, what then?' Also, consider using the Tool AT2 Resourceful Spaces technique if they are finding it difficult to psychologically dissociate.

Using other tools

Consider Tool PL1 Logical Wheels and Tool PL2 Time Trail.

2 Authenticity Profile

Introduction

This tool is designed to enable the coachee to reflect upon, and track, progress to become more authentic in their work (and in other aspects of their life). Authenticity can be defined as, 'being true to who we are and what we believe to be important'. It is characterized by actions and thoughts that are consistent with a high level of self-esteem. This tool identifies and enables the coachee to track five elements of their own authenticity.

Learning outcomes

- Have reflected upon your current level of authenticity in a semi-quantitative way.
- Create a reference score to enable you to track changes in your authenticity.
- Devise behavioural goals to develop aspects of your own authenticity.

Triggers

Coachees who say one or more of these types of phrases:

- I am having trouble feeling genuine when working with co-workers.
- The organization is not very open.
- I don't think much of myself at work.
- I feel like I am leading two lives.

Underpinning rationale

Authenticity is underpinned by self-esteem. The tool develops an understanding of five aspects of self-esteem. People can improve their authenticity by breaking it down into sub-aspects and setting goals. This challenges our beliefs around what they can and cannot say, think or do. These can then bring about positive improvements in relationships, rapport and the quality of working with others and so also affect productivity. Additionally, raised authenticity can make a positive contribution towards confidence in any setting, including work.

Instructions for use

Complete the tracker (Table 7.2) and total up the scores for each table (Tables 7.3–7.6). Calculate an overall score and plot it on the tracker. You can then set goals in one or more areas and repeat the tracker questionnaire later and periodically.

Five aspects of authenticity

Authenticity can be defined as being true to who we are and what we believe to be important. It is a vital way of 'being' at work if we are to be believable to colleagues. Authenticity is closely linked to high levels of self-esteem and to strong senses of both purpose and mission in our work. Authenticity can be sub-divided into five aspects which are summarized below in the acronym VALUE:

Values and vision – have an explicit awareness of what's important and where you are heading.

Align to live with integrity – live in line with values and beliefs.

Live in the 'now' – being aware of what we are doing and thinking as we are living. This is the so-called reflexive thinking that enables us to be 'present' and pick up what is really being said and done both around us, and within us.

Understand and accept – accept who we are and take responsibility for our own thoughts, feelings and actions. Learn to take responsibility for changing things we have control and influence over and accept what cannot be changed, so that we can move on.

Efficacy – be the architect of your own destiny and outcomes, decide what is right and make it happen.

Authenticity tracker

TABLE 7.2 Values and vision tracker

Emerging	Embedded			
	1	2	3	4
I have clearly defined what is important in my work				
I can talk confidently about my current top five values in each area of my wheel of work, e.g. career progression, work–life balance, job satisfaction, relationships, etc.				
I have a clear sense of purpose in my work				
I have clarity of vision about the future I desire				
I have a clear set of principles that I work to, in making decisions				
Total:				

Note: This table is downloadable at www.performancecoachingtoolkit.com.

TABLE 7.3 Align to live with integrity tracker

Emerging	Embedded			
	1	2	3	4
I take confident decisions to stay **aligned** with what I believe in				
I have difficult conversations when they are necessary in order to stay aligned with my values				
I state my position and make it clear to others even if the prevailing direction is away from what I feel is important				
I am willing to accommodate the views and values of others in situations where I cannot have ultimate control over direction and approach				
Total:				

Note: This table is downloadable at www.performancecoachingtoolkit.com.

TABLE 7.4 Live in the NOW tracker

Emerging	Embedded			
	1	2	3	4
I pay attention to conversations as they are happening, listening carefully to the views of others				
I am actively aware of my own responses to the viewpoints and actions of others				
I am fully open to the feedback that others might offer in relation to my work, conduct, beliefs and direction				
I strike an accurate balance between what goes on around me and what goes on inside my own consciousness				
Total:				

Note: This table is downloadable at www.performancecoachingtoolkit.com.

TABLE 7.5 Understand and accept tracker

Emerging	Embedded			
	1	2	3	4
I am able to move from feeling emotions to being sufficiently dissociated from them to be rational in my responses				
I am able to apply my values and principles to support the wider good in complex situations				
I recognize when my ego interferes with effectiveness				
I am able to exert control over my ego to maintain balanced decision-making				
Total:				

Note: This table is downloadable at www.performancecoachingtoolkit.com.

TABLE 7.6 Efficacy tracker

Emerging	Embedded			
	1	2	3	4
I am the architect of my destiny				
I take full responsibility for my own choices and actions				
I take responsibility for my own happiness				
I take actions that improve the degree of control and influence I have over my life				
I empower others to exert control over their lives I take appropriate action on the things				
I have control over				
I accept the things I cannot change in my life and move on				
Total:				

Note: This table is downloadable at www.performancecoachingtoolkit.com.

Where do you go from here?

Within the tool

Once the tracker is complete, coaches can encourage coachees to look at:

- areas of strength;

- areas for development;

- realistic target-setting for developing authenticity;

- as a baseline for probing unhelpful beliefs, for example, 'What causes you to hold back in meetings? What do you believe will happen if you put your points across for a second time?'

Using other tools

Use any of the other tools from the Perception section of the toolkit (pp. 100–26) to support the re-evaluation of limiting thinking.

3 Feedback

Introduction

Feedback helps to correct a misunderstanding and brings new awareness to perceptions (including self). Feedback helps to bring conscious awareness to limiting patterns of thinking and/or behaviour. Feedback is primarily for the coachee's benefit but of course, the coach will also learn much faster by requesting feedback at the end of each session. Feedback may also be given where an existing and useful coachee-pattern can be applied successfully in another context. Most often, this will be established by routine questioning in order to seek positive references from their own learning (from the coaching interventions).

Learning outcomes

- Understanding why feedback is so useful to well-being and success.
- Have an acceptable model for giving feedback.

Triggers

- Awareness by the coach of dysfunctional patterns of thinking or behaviour in the coachee.
- The coachee is limited by their beliefs or their unproductive thinking patterns (and where other more useful beliefs and patterns have already been established in another context).

Underpinning rationale

Feedback drives self-awareness and provides opportunity for self-managing change. Feedback is based upon facts and observable behaviours and is likely to be received more productively by the coachee than offering vague opinions. Feedback describing the current situation as well as a future scenario (where the feedback has been acted on by the coachee) provides a push–pull motivation for change.

Instructions for use

Use *TIDI* as an aide-mémoire when giving feedback:

- **T**hinking pattern or behaviour identified
- **I**mpact on me/us
- **D**esired behaviours
- **I**mpact on me/us which will result.

Example

T I notice that you have arrived a few minutes late for each of our last three sessions.

I I could take that as an indication that you may not really want to be here and I wonder if other people would think that, if this is something you do from time to time.

D I would prefer to see you arrive on time when possible.

I If and when you do that, I would feel more comfortable and I hope that you might also enjoy the first few minutes better, as we renew our working relationship and prepare for the new session.

Example

Where a coachee is providing evidence of an existing and more positive pattern, the coach's conversation may be more like this:

T I think I notice two distinct reactions from you when faced with challenge. The first is what you did just now, to laugh or make a joke, sometimes in a way that is self-disparaging.

I When you do that, it undermines my confidence in you being successful.

D On other occasions, for example, when we talked about the upcoming conference, you have been immediately focused, alert, leaning forward, concentrating. I wonder if you could notice your own reactions to challenge and if you wanted, to choose to adopt the more alert reaction?

I When you do react with alertness and focus, I feel that you are fully engaged and am confident that you will be successful. I am sure other people would have similar reactions also.

Where do you go from here?

Within the tool

Ask a question like, 'Is this feedback useful to you and if it stimulates a desire for action, what is that action now?' This may be followed by another, 'The process of coaching builds success upon success and therefore all actions need to be as certain as possible to be successful ones. How are you sure that you will be successful?'

Using other tools

Where the issue has complexity, it may be necessary to drill down to establish root cause or to identify the earliest possible trigger for the pattern. Tool S1 the Pattern Breaker may be helpful. Anchoring new patterns to the trigger can be productive. Techniques to achieve this may include Tool PE10 SWISH, but only if the coachee has good visual and **kinaesthetic** intelligences.

PE

4 Devil's Advocate

Introduction

B old statements of limiting belief about the world are great opportunities for change. Using the Devil's Advocate tool can help galvanize a change in perception for the better.

Learning outcomes

Knowing when to use the Devil's Advocate's intervention and how to apply it.

Triggers

All the triggers infer lack of energy to action. The triggers are often subconscious or subliminal excuses for failing.

- It's always like that.
- Well, one would expect a woman to be treated like that.
- The people who came from the last take-over company always do better here.

Underpinning rationale

Statements of limiting belief may be unrealistic and undermine the confidence and motivation of an individual to action. Exploring reasoned argument from another perspective can lead to a healthier perception. These new perceptions produce more holistic understandings of 'how things work around here' and to more motivated and considered action, instead of inaction. The Devil's Advocate intervention is one good way to start that process.

Instructions for use

The Devil's Advocate intervention from the coach takes the form: 'And if you were to be a remote and all-seeing observer, could you argue exactly the opposite view, in a reasoned way?'

Follow-up questions will seek to explore and expand perceptions so that the bold 'fact' is undermined and a new and more reasonable statement obtained from the coachee. The coach might also ask these questions:

- So it does not always have to be like that? What are the factors determining the outcome?
- Knowing that, what specifically could you do now to be more certain of a successful outcome?
- Earlier, if I heard you correctly, you said that 'it's always like that' so how would you describe your impression now?

Where do you go from here?

Within the tool

The coachee is sometimes slow to understand what is required of them as they may have had no similar experience of opposing their own statements in their life before. So further and more explicit statement and question may be needed, for example: 'If I heard you right, you said that "it's always like that" in relation to how the managers in your organization deal with pregnant women. If you were to be a Devil's Advocate, you would believe and adopt the opposite view. You would look for any signs that, what you have described earlier, is not always the case and that there are variances in what happens.'

Other options for starting the process of challenge instead of the Devil's Advocate include these:

- Who says?
- That's an interesting view, how do you come by that exactly?
- Always? Can you think now of an exception?

Using other tools

Having shifted their view of the world, there may be new options for action and these will need exploration. Tool PA1 the Ranking Question can be used both for logical calibration but also so the coachee can compare and contrast their emotional responses to differing scenarios and perspectives. A **SWOT analysis** might also prove useful.

5 Leader and Follower

Introduction

Where there is a frustrated target or an obvious block to progress, this tool provides a route for the coachee to touch the resource from motivations and de-motivations. This process can provide a mechanism for unblocking issues and creating success.

Learning outcomes

Draws out what is important for motivated success.

Triggers

- I'm not sure I can do that . . .
- I want that but . . .
- If only I . . .

Underpinning rationale

There is invariably something behind positive drive and also something behind a blockage to progress. When these are both made conscious, it is possible to move forward.

Instructions for use

The model relies on the repetitive use of two questions, the so-called 'leader question', 'So, what does <that> do for you?' and the so-called 'follower question', 'And what stops you <from>'? Both questions are typically used in conjunction with the coachee's own words (from their previous response). For example, here is the leader question in practical use:

Angus: *What does* the promotion *do for you?*
Jon: More money and self-direction.
Angus: And *what does* more money and more self-direction *do for you?*

Jon:	Greater freedom of choice.
Angus:	And *what does* greater freedom of choice *do for you*?
Jon:	It's a feeling of well-being.
Angus:	And this feeling of well-being, *what does* that feeling of well-being *do for you*?
Jon:	I feel taller, cooler, happier.
Angus:	And, when having a feeling of well-being, when you are feeling taller, cooler, happier, *what does* feeling taller, cooler, happier *do for you*?
Jon:	I get . . . I have a warm feeling inside my chest that lifts and fills me.
Angus:	And this warm feeling that is inside your chest is lifting and filling you, so *what does* that *do for you*?
Jon:	It's the best way to be.
Angus:	And this best way to be, *what does* this 'best way to be' *do for you*?
Jon:	I can do anything.
Angus:	And this best way to be when you can do anything, *what does* that 'I can do anything' *do for you*?
Jon:	That's it! When I have this warm feeling, I feel I can do anything!

Here is the follower question in use:

Angus:	Jon, you said you want to apply for the new job. So, *what stops you*?
Jon:	I do not want to let my boss down *and* I am nervous about what it will be like to fail my application.

Here is the first line of questioning for the first of the two issues mentioned:

Angus:	*What stops you* going for the new job AND not letting your boss down?
Jon:	I can seek his advice and support and anyway leave my post in good order.
Angus:	So, *what stops you* doing that?
Jon:	Nothing.

Angus started the second line of questioning:

Angus:	*What stops you* feeling okay if your application fails?
Jon:	Losing face with colleagues.
Angus:	Your application has failed, so *what stops you* keeping face with your colleagues?
Jon:	Lack of bravado.
Angus:	*What stops you* having more bravado?
Jon:	Nothing. If I thought about it, I can do it. I will tell people what I am doing and why, how I think my chances are and I will discuss some of the consequences for me of winning or losing the appointment.
Angus:	Do you have some actions then?

Where do you go from here?

Within the tool

The coachee is invariably now ready to get to action. The coach will need to be disciplined to select any of the STEPPPA tools (PL) that lead to Plan and then Pace to ensure that their target has the best possible chance of success.

PE

6 Polarity Coaching

Introduction

The novice coach will often tend to follow 'positive' leads from the coachee as these seem to be good in their world-view. Motivation, however, is more complex than this and is achieved by carrots and by sticks, by both the *positive* and by any distaste for the *negative*. The coach needs discipline to make sure that the opposite aspect of information is explored by the coachee.

Learning outcomes

Understand how using polarity coaching heightens the push towards achieving goals in coachees.

Triggers

- I am not sure what to do.
- I am not really that bothered.

Also triggered by lack of authenticity between body language and verbal language, for example, 'I am totally up for that', said with low energy and head down.

Underpinning rationale

Coachees give us their own clues to both their motivations and their limiting beliefs almost every time they speak. Polarity-based coaching capitalizes on their motivational energy, both carrots and sticks. When using polarity, it is often usual to encourage the coachee to explore their experience of what they have just said in depth before moving to the other extreme, their polarity, of their experience. Exploring the extremes of thinking expands the view that a coachee has of their situation and helps them to contextualize, including a wider range of understanding and motivation into their situation.

Instructions for use

This particular tool is best illustrated through examples. Here are examples with one or two coaching replies that might be used later. In each case, the coach might refer back by saying, 'If I heard you correctly, you said earlier that, "I'm quite okay with that", so, I wonder now, what are you not quite so okay with?'

A general process for polarity Coaching is also presented. Copy it and use it when you need to.

Coachee: I'm quite okay with that.
Coach: What are you not quite so okay with? Calibrate 'quite okay' for me.

Coachee: That would be great!
Coach: And, if that does not happen?
Coachee: It wouldn't be so bad.
Coach: How bad could it be? Can you influence that?

Coachee: I want to do this now.
Coach: And, if you don't?

Coachee: They think I'm great!
Coach: What would make them think less of you? Is there a cost to being thought of as great?

Coachee: It's a horrid situation.
Coach: And is there an opposite experience in this situation that you can have? How horrid is horrid and can you influence that?

Note that the polarity does not introduce the coach's interpretations. The language of the coach reflects that of the *coachee*, or you could have this happening:

Coachee: I've decided to train as a helicopter pilot.
Coach: What would it be like to guide caving expeditions?
Coachee: I hate being in confined, dark spaces.

In each case, the coach needs to think about the coachee's 'experience' and encourage them to explore their own polarities in relation to that, not the coach's polarities!

A general process for polarity coaching

1   State what you think you've heard.

2   Formulate an opposite challenge in one of the following forms:

   (a)   Feed in an opposite directly, for example, flying to caving
   (b)   What is the opposite of this?
   (c)   If that experience were on a line at one end, what would be at the other?
   (d)   Offer a resourcing question which might be in one of the following forms: What

can you control or influence here?; What can you do?; or What will the consequences be?

Note: This resource is available to download at www.performancecoachingtoolkit.com.

Where do you go from here?

Within the tool

Continue to explore the polarity dimension to the coachee's statement with curious questioning to draw out their specific learning. Facilitate their learning to help them establish what general rules they could now apply in similar situations.

Using other tools

Alternative approaches to this can be found in Tool PE5 Leader and Follower. Other ways of shifting perception that might also be useful include Tool PE4 Devil's Advocate and Tool PE1 Objective Advice.

7 Perceptual Positions – Second Position

PE

Introduction

This tool is useful where a coachee has a misunderstanding about another person's mindset and motives, or where another person is in conflict with the coachee.

Learning outcomes

The tool offers the coachee a fresh perspective on the possible thinking, feeling and motivations *of another person*. It provides an opportunity for the coachee to do something differently to change the quality of the interaction they have with that person.

Triggers

- I don't understand where she is coming from.
- He is just getting at me all the time.
- Why would anyone do that?

Underpinning rationale

- That a new and alternative perspective can provide ammunition for change.

- The coachee's learning can be wrong but the learning can and does, often, create positive change.

Instructions for use

Ask the coachee to think of a recent and typical event when they have been with the person. Ask them for a name or pseudonym that they are happy to use to represent that person. Say something like, 'Sometimes it is useful to get a real experience of being in the other person's shoes, to really enter into the whole experience of being them, looking like them and to feel like them in that situation. Before you do that, you might like to think about how to organize that in this space here and who is located where in the room. Then, at a moment of your own choice, for you to move back in time, spin the clock back and notice that place in the room where <name the other person> is standing or sitting. As you are moving to that place and becoming them, in that situation, the clock is spinning back and you are taking on all you know about them, their age, gender, physical movements and health.'

Shadow the coachee unobtrusively as they move. You should see physical changes arising from their change of psychological state. Ask, 'So, <name of other person>, what is going on here?' Follow this with a number of questions to elicit information, for example, 'So, <name of other person>' then continue as below:

- What is <name the coachee> wanting from you?
- What do you want from <name of coachee>?
- How can you both compromise or collaborate to reach a workable solution?
- What would make you feel more confident/happy about <name of coachee>?
- If you had a real gift of advice for <name of coachee> that would make this situation better for you now, what would that advice be?

Make a mental (or quietly written) note of the exact form of words they use. If the form of words is lengthy ask this, 'So, <name of person> if you had to put that advice in a nutshell now, what is that nutshell of advice?' Make a precise record or mental note of that advice. Then, to get them back, say, 'In a moment <name of person>, I want you to move over there <pointing to where the coachee first started> and when you do that, to allow the clock to spin forward so that by the time you get there, you will be <name of coachee> again. And you will be in the coaching space with <name of coach>.' Shadow them and ask some questions, if necessary, to be sure they are fully back in a state of readiness for coaching by asking logical questions, moving their attention to you or elsewhere in the room.

Say, 'Now, I have very good advice for you. It really is the best possible advice available at the moment and it is this . . .' The coach then relays the advice precisely and with the same tone and intonation (as used earlier). Leave a silent space for that advice to be integrated. If the coachee goes into a reflective psychological state and then starts to fidget or look bored, repeat the previous sentence again. This should take them back instantly to that reflective, silent space. Typically the coachee will then provide some information or insight.

Where do you go from here?

Within the tool

If they did not gain significant learning, it may be that their ability, or flexibility to change their psychological state at will, is not particularly developed. To check, ask, 'So, what if anything do you take from that experience?', or ask, 'So, zero to ten, how well do you think you became that person as a real experience of being them, where ten is perfectly being them?' If the coachee confirms a weakness in this ability, it is not a reason for the coach to give up. Rather, if the coach can convince the coachee that this ability could be useful to them, to offer them the tool as homework.

Using other tools

If they are able to manage their state creatively, you can consider using Tool PE8 Perceptual Positions – Third Position (observer position) to provide further insights. These insights come from a more detached (less emotionally involved) perspective. This is particularly useful if the coachee is any way distressed by what has been happening in the relationship and/or the effect of that.

8 Perceptual Positions – Third Position

Introduction

This tool is useful where a coachee has a misunderstanding about another person's mindset and motives, or where another person is in conflict with the coachee. It is often used as an adjunct to the use of the second (perceptual) position, but also where a detached view is helpful because the whole recall about that relationship is stressful – and the coachee is emotionally affected to the extent that they are unable to make logical progress.

Learning outcomes

The tool offers the coachee another perspective on the dynamic within the relationship between the coachee and the other person. It can also offer specific insights about the thinking, feeling and motivations of that other person. It provides an opportunity for the coachee to do something differently to change the quality of the interaction they have with that person.

Triggers

- Thanks for the idea of second positioning her, but I hate her too much to want to try and 'be' her.
- I am too upset to talk about this (and the coachee will appear emotionally affected).

Underpinning rationale

- That a new and alternative perspective can provide ammunition for change.

- It provides an alternative rational or clinical perspective, which is more free from debilitating emotions associated with recall.

- The coachee's learning can be wrong but the learning can, and often does, create positive change.

Instructions for use

Ask the coachee to think of a recent and typical event when they have been with the person. Ask them for a name or pseudonym that they are happy to use to represent that person. Say something like, 'Sometimes it is useful to get an experience of being totally detached from the situation to get a clear and clinical view of what is happening when you two are together, would you like to do that?' If they agree, say something like, 'Before you do that, you might like to think about how to organize this space. Who is situated where in the room? At a moment of your own choice, move back in time, and place yourself remotely from both <name of coachee> and <name or other person>. Make sure that you are far enough away so that you can observe with total detachment. Some people find it useful to imagine looking through a special telescope, so you can see what is happening from a long way away but you can hear any conversation, if you choose to do so. As you will be moving to that remote, clinical, observer place, the clock will be spinning back and you will become more clinical and aware of both of them.' Shadow the coachee unobtrusively as they move. You should see physical changes typical of emotional detachment in them. Ask, 'So, what is going on with them?' Follow this with a number of questions like those below and start each question like this, 'So, you are a remote observer . . .'

- What does <name of the other person> think of <name of coachee>?
- How does <name of the other person> interpret what <Name of coachee> is saying?
- What does <name of the other person> want from <name of coachee>?
- If there was a real gift of advice from <name of the other person> for <name of coachee>, what would that advice be now?

Make a mental (or quietly written) note of the exact form of words they use. If the form of words is lengthy ask this, 'So, if you had to put that advice in a nutshell now, what is that nutshell of advice?' Make a precise record or mental note of that advice. To get them back, say, 'In a moment I want you to move over there <pointing to where the coachee first started> and when you do that, allow the clock to spin forward so that by the time you get there, you will again be <name of coachee> and in the coaching space with <name of coach>.'

Shadow them and ask some questions, if necessary, to be sure they are fully back in a state of readiness for coaching by asking logical questions, moving their attention to you or elsewhere in the room.

Say, 'Now, I have very good advice for you. It really is the best possible advice available at the moment and it is this . . .' The coach then relays the advice precisely and with the same tone and intonation (as used earlier). Leave a silent space for that advice to be integrated. If the coachee goes into a reflective psychological state and, later, starts to fidget or look bored, repeat the previous sentence again. This should take them back instantly to that reflective, silent space. Typically the coachee will then provide some information or insight.

Where do you go from here?

Within the tool

Think about using Tool CT6 Reflective Language to help the coachee stay in (psychological) state. Practise changing to the present tense when the coachee has moved to another perceptual position. Practise recalling advice from perceptual positions precisely and with accurate tonality and pace.

Using other tools

If the coachee has been poor at experiencing the Third Perceptual Position then you might encourage them to practise doing this exercise at home. If they are able to manage their state creatively in this way, then you can consider using Tool PE7 the Second Perceptual Position (if that is not unduly distressing for them) as this can provide further insights. Other homework could include asking them to really imagine that they are experiencing a recent holiday again and to make that experience as real as possible by using their imagination. This will prepare them for other imaginative psychological work and help them to be more amenable to the coaching experience.

PE

9 The 51% Rule

Introduction

The 51% Rule of McLeod (2006: 82) is particularly useful to a coachee who is prevaricating over an issue of communication/relationship with another person.

Learning outcomes

● Understand the 51% Rule.
● Know when and how to introduce the model to a coachee.

Triggers

● I'm in a stalemate situation with them.
● They should say sorry first.
● Surely, they should make the first move.

Underpinning rationale

'In any given interaction with another person, I am 51 per cent responsible for that interaction.' If the coachee is less than 50 per cent responsible then they would probably do nothing. If the coachee was 100 per cent responsible, then they might exhibit neurotic behaviours at work and may keep interfering in matters that do not directly concern them. By helping the coachee to establish their responsibility at 51 per cent, the onus is on them to act and not let the issue stew. The rule reduces the possibility of 'stalemate' since action invariably follows. This rule is simply a device, or tool, to encourage new perception.

Instructions for use

Offering coachees the 51% Rule provides them with a simple and memorable fix for situations where there is stalemate. Once they take on board the idea that they are 51 per cent responsible for any given interaction, then stalemate is impossible; action invariably follows. The actions themselves may not give the expected outcome, but will usually change the situation for the better.

In all cases, the coachee should determine whether the tool is suitable for them:

Coach: There is a tool that may be useful to you <wait for reaction>. It's called the 51% Rule. Have you heard of it and would you like to know about it?

Coachee: If you think it helpful.

Coach: The rule says that in any given interaction with another person, you are 51 per cent responsible for that interaction. In the situation you have been describing, does the idea offer any ideas that may be useful?

Coachee: I will not wait for her to take action, I will do so myself. I will make it clear that the relationship with her is more important that the issue alone and will ask her to participate in finding a compromise, one that we can both live with. If she will not engage, then at least I have tried to resolve the situation and would then let my line manager know what I have done, just for the record.

Where do you go from here?

Within the tool

Check for commitment for example, using Tool PA1 the Ranking Question.

Using other tools

Think about resourcing from the future, for example, a Time Trail (p. 138). Often, when the coachee is struggling with relationship issues, the Perceptual Positions tools (Tools PE7 and PE8) are helpful.

10 SWISH

Introduction

Use SWISH with someone who has a repeated, patterned and negative experience which they want to replace with a more positive, resourceful psychological state, or mindset. To use SWISH, they must be inherently flexible in their visual intelligence and be able to play with psychological images. It also depends upon the coachee having a real emotional association with both their current psychological pattern (in visual representation) and real emotional association with a preferred state. SWISH deploys 'habitual association' to automatically create the second, desired experience when it is triggered by the first.

Learning outcomes

- An automatic, new and positive response to an event/stimulus that, up until now, had a negative experience associated with it.
- Development of improved visual acuity including 'visual constructs' as well as the ability to psychologically associate desired, kinaesthetic (feeling) experiences with those images, offering the coachee further developmental opportunities.

Triggers

- I'm frightened of . . .
- I'm always unhappy when . . .
- I'm waiting for something bad to happen.
- When I (experience or do something) I feel (something negative) for example, even in this room, if I see something moving in the corner of my eye, I immediately know/feel that it is a snake.

Underpinning rationale

We can often re-pattern automatic (negative) reactions to life-experiences using visual imagery. Creative, visual imagery coupled with repeated, kinaesthetic experiences can change phobic reactions to triggering stimuli.

Instructions for use

Unless you are already very aware of the coachee's significant visual intelligence, try and test that by asking, 'If I was to ask you to recall a pleasant experience from your last holiday, could you do that by seeing that in your mind's eye? And when you do that, could you change anything in that picture, for example, the colours? Could you also change the temperature of the air on your body?' If the coachee is able to do this, you can explain why you had asked them those questions and then introduce SWISH to them. If they are not flexible in the use of these skills, encourage their development by suggesting they do homework to enhance their skills. Here are the SWISH coaching steps:

1   The coachee is invited to enter the (psychological) state that they 'dislike' by returning to a recent event and seeing the (cue) image (within a border) and experiencing that as completely as they can. When complete, invite the coachee to 'clear the screen'. Ask them how perfectly they are able to do this on a scale of zero to ten, where ten is perfect. If they give you a value below 8, ask them how perfectly they believe they could do this with practice. Ask them also how perfectly, zero to ten, someone else with excellent visual skills could do this if they practised a lot. This number is then probably their recalibrated maximum.[1] This question helps to recalibrate that answer. Repeat the image exercise until they are achieving scores that are close to the recalibrated maximum.

2   Invite the coachee to imagine a nice picture (target image) of how they would like their experience to be. The coach encourages the coachee to alter that experience towards an even more comfortable and positive experience using illumination, colour, brightness, tone, back-lighting, distance and texture, for example. This is repeated, as above.

3   Explain that the 'target image' will be shrunk down into the corner of the 'cue image' and that the target image will expand and brighten at the same moment that the cue image darkens and fades away. The coachee does this and is then asked whether this new experience is as powerful as that reached in step 2.

4   The coachee repeats step 3 more rapidly to the word 'SWISH' and their response is checked after repeating a few times.

5   The coachee is asked to imagine a future time when a similar event could trigger their experience again. If the SWISH does not work, repeat steps 1 to 4 again.

Where do you go from here?

Within the tool

Consider other preliminary work that requires psychological agility including visual exercises. A coachee may find this tiring, so be sure to attend to their psychological state and adapt as necessary.

Using other tools

Offer homework in order that the coachee plays with images in more creative ways[2] and Time Trail (p. 138).

Notes

1 Coachees often recalibrate 10 maximum and replace with a lower number between 6 and 9, most typically, 8.
2 In NLP terms, this process uses 'sub-modalities'. A sub-modality is NLP-speak for variations in cognitive experience.

Further reading

McLeod, A. (2003) *Performance Coaching: The Handbook for Managers, HR Professionals and Coaches.* Carmarthen and New York: Crown House Publishing.
McDermott, I. and Jago, W. (2003) *The NLP Coach.* London: Piatkus.
Zeus, P. and Skiffington, S. (2002) *The Coaching at Work Toolkit.* Maidenhead: McGraw-Hill.

CHAPTER 8

PLan Focus in STEPPPA

1 Logical Wheels

Introduction

This tool is a combination of two well-used concepts in coaching. The wheel of life (and wheel of work) together with the '**logical levels**' of Gregory Bateson (1972) and adapted by Dilts (1990: 56). These come together here to create an ideal starting point for both coaching and for self-coaching.

Learning outcomes

- Relative levels of contentment in eight areas of the coachee's work.
- Awareness of new and useful emergent patterns in relation to work strengths and challenges.
- Deeper insight into each of the eight work areas using a range of questions which probe at varying levels of professional and personal development.

Triggers

A starting point for a coaching conversation or for a series of conversations. The coachee saying:

- I have so much going on at work, I don't know where to begin in order to sort things out.

- Everything is fine, there's nothing to talk about.
- I'd like to get going and make some changes, but it's complicated.

Underpinning rationale

If one can break down one's working life into a series of aspects, then one can step back and identify areas for development. The potential to generate goals and the strategies for achieving those result in a performance improvement. The tool encourages coachees to explore aspects of their work performance at a number of different levels using the logical levels model (Table 8.1). Questions are designed to challenge the coachee's concept of what is happening at the different levels.

TABLE 8.1 Logical levels

Logical level	Description
Purpose	Your mission – your purpose for doing what you do
Identity	Who you are and who you are being
Beliefs and values	What you believe and what you believe is important
Capabilities	Your skills, attributes and knowledge
Environment	The practical boundaries and constraints within your environment

Dilts suggested that there is a hierarchy to these levels in relation to problem-solving. In order to solve a problem at a particular level, one must work at a level that is at least on, or above, the level at which the problem formed. For example, if your office is not big enough for your needs (environment), you might need to develop a tighter set of organizing skills or influence your boss to give you a bigger one (operate at capabilities level).

Instructions for use

Invite your coachee to work around the eight elements of the Wheel of Work (Figure 8.1), giving each area a score out of 10 for 'contentment' (where 1 is not at all contented, and 10 is totally content).

Once this has been completed, open up a discussion about the wheel and what it reveals to them. Some useful questions are:

- What does it reveal?
- What does it confirm?
- What surprises you?
- If there was another area which you could add to the wheel, what would that be and what score would you give to it?
- Are there any patterns that emerge?
- If you could change one area right now, which would it be and why?

FIGURE 8.1 Wheel of work for logical wheels

Once you have encouraged this reflection, invite your coachee to pick an area (or areas) they most want to work on. Then, use the area-specific logical wheel (Figure 8.2) to promote further exploration. Feel free to probe with further questions and assist the coachee to summarize the key learning and actions emerging from each area discussed.

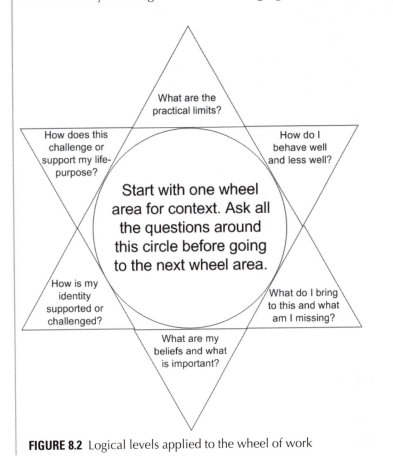

FIGURE 8.2 Logical levels applied to the wheel of work

In situations where coachees may feel that many or all areas of the wheel are worthy of work, you could offer the following approaches:

- Pick one area that, if it improved, would have the most positive impact on the other areas.
- Pick an area to begin with and work around the wheel in any direction.
- Pick the area you feel you could get an immediate benefit from.
- Pick the area that you have least wanted to discuss.

Now look at the areas of the wheel of work in Figure 8.1 again. Match the relevant slice of the wheel of work to the logical wheel questions in Figures 8.3–8.10. Go through the questions in the logical wheels and apply them to the coachee's particular context, as shown in the centre of the logical wheels in Figures 8.3–8.10. Record the coachee's responses and ascertain what this tells you about the coachee.

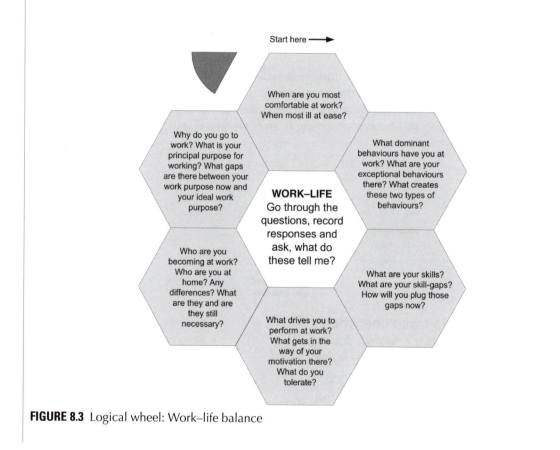

FIGURE 8.3 Logical wheel: Work–life balance

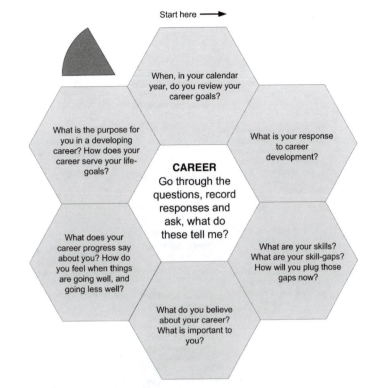

FIGURE 8.4 Logical wheel: Career progression

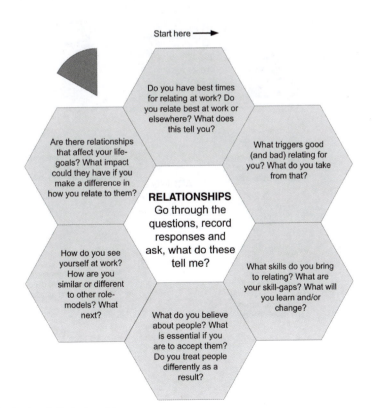

FIGURE 8.5 Logical wheel: Relationships

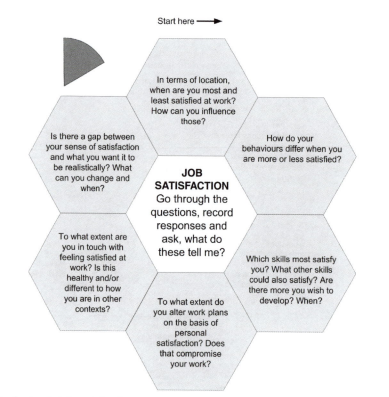

FIGURE 8.6 Logical wheel: Job satisfaction

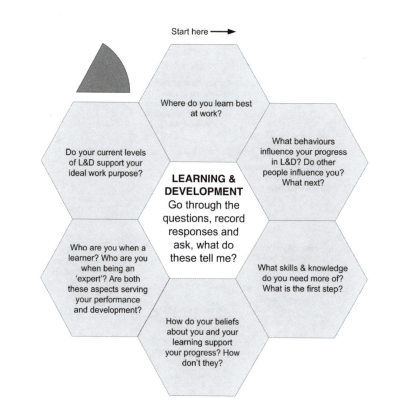

FIGURE 8.7 Logical wheel: Learning and development

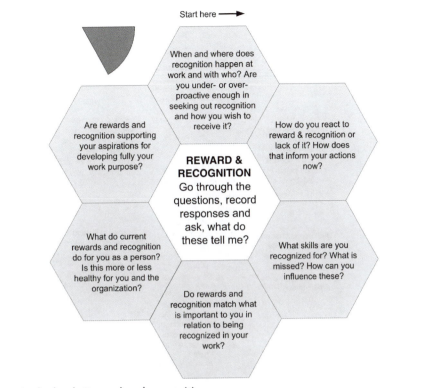

FIGURE 8.8 Logical wheel: Reward and recognition

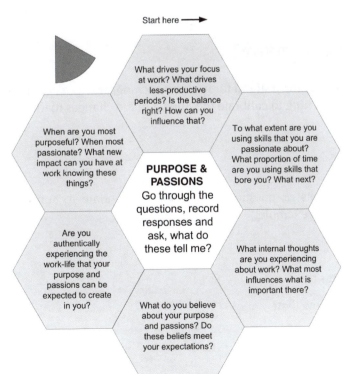

FIGURE 8.9 Logical wheel: Purpose and passions

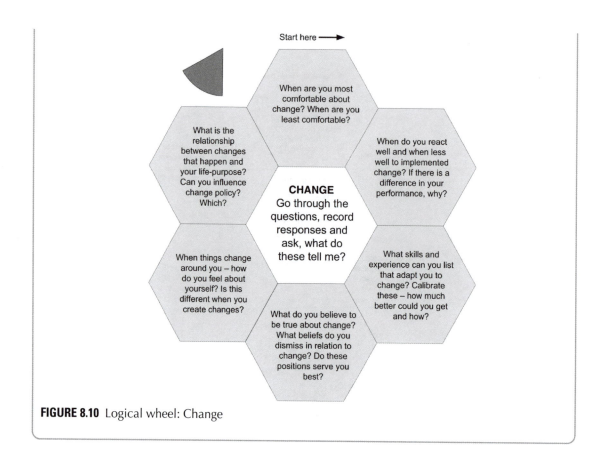

FIGURE 8.10 Logical wheel: Change

Where do you go from here?

Each area can then become a strand for further coaching. The tool can be re-run at the end of a defined period of coaching to calibrate the impact of the changes made.

Within the tool

Use any other prompts or questions that seem appropriate to support and challenge the coachee's thinking, for example:

- What's next?
- Who says that's true?
- How do you know that?
- What's the evidence for that?
- So what?
- Who could help you?

Using other tools

Consider using Time Trail (p. 138), Tool PA1 the Ranking Question and Tool PA3 Letting Go.

2 Time Trail

Introduction

Time Trail uses a person's subconscious representation of time as if it were a line running from past, to present and then to future. The concept holds that all life experiences and their associated emotions can be represented unconsciously, along the trail or path. This representation can then be accessed and used to draw positive learning from 'future' events. It can release any negative emotions associated with these possible future events.

Learning outcomes

- Coachees gain useful insights into any negative projections they may have about their future.
- Coachees learn to anticipate potential future challenges in advance.
- They can then devise strategies to assist them in meeting those challenges.

Triggers

The coachee may say:

- I feel anxious about the interview next week.
- I am determined to stay calm about the court case, but every time I think about it, I break out in a cold sweat.
- I feel uncertain about the future as redundancies look likely.

Underpinning rationale

A coachee can usefully visualize a footpath or trail in the direction of their future in order to prepare psychologically and emotionally for a future event. A coachee can then float aside from the trail, or above it, to create emotional distance from the trail (and the associated events that would otherwise affect them negatively). This dissociation from the 'unpleasant' can help a coachee to **reframe** their attitude to real events in the future. The tool permits the coachee to find out what the experience of 'going beyond' such an event is like. From this, a coachee can gain insights and motivation to face the future.

Instructions for use

Scripted tool

Stage 1

You can use this script to help facilitate your coachee:

1   We can use a method of dealing with your possible future, negative prospect, to help you with your challenge around <use their words to describe their challenge>.

2   First of all, I would like to help you understand that you have a conscious and a sub-conscious capability to process information. Your conscious capacity includes all the things that you are know about, for example, your ability to rationalize and converse inside your mind, to take conscious decisions. Equally you have an unconscious mind which is responsible for processing emotions, taking care of your survival and remembering and organizing all of your experiences.

3   I expect that you organize time in a particular way. You might like to try organizing time, past, present and future, so that it is arranged in a line somewhere of your choosing. Perhaps that line will be from front to back or from side to side or from top to bottom, or some other variation on those.

4   In a moment, I am going to ask you to trust your instinct and to point in the direction of your past. Would you do that when you are ready? <Coach notes direction.>

5   I am now going to ask you to point in the direction of your future. Would you do that when you are ready? <Coach notes direction.>

6   Where is 'now' located?

7   Good, now we are going to work with your future line to assist you in dealing with your issue <use coachee's descriptor>.

Stage 2

1   Now, I would like you to close your eyes and as you do that, find that you can locate your future time trail, and as you do that, describe how it looks or feels or what you can hear as you are becoming more and more aware of the path you have in your mind. <Allow the coachee time to describe their experience of their trail.>

2   OK, with your eyes still closed, you can choose how you will be working with your trail. You might like to float up above it, or move beside the trail and experience it from there. You will be able to go where you want, provided that you can still experience your trail. <Allow the coachee a short time to choose, then ask what they have decided.>

3   Good, now we will stay around 'NOW' on your trail, but play with moving away from that place. So, in your own time, move away from the trail in whichever direction you have decided is good for you, say 20 metres or so and when you are ready, slide back

towards the trail around NOW. Now take yourself away from the trail so far that you can see the beginning, the 'now' and the future of the trail. It becomes so far away that it is indistinct now, but you can still sense the essence of what is going on during that time journey. When you are ready, in your time, return to 'now' and open your eyes.

Stage 3

1   In this final step, I invite you to close your eyes again and in your mind, once more, to move a long way from your trail until you are at a comfortable distance.

2   When you are ready, keep your distance but travel past the end of the future, perhaps some minutes or so after it is all over.

3   Now that you are beyond your successful event, move slowly back to the trail and to that time and in your mind's eye, experience fully what it is like to be here, in this success. <The coach can make that experience more real by asking present tense questions about their awareness.>

4   Now what positive learning do you have from the trail?

5   Invite the coachee to come back into the room.

Where do you go from here?

Within the tool

This tool becomes a way of resolving emotional difficulties. It is important to ensure that coachees dissociate with appropriate distance from their experiences on the Time Trail. A high degree of assertiveness on the part of the coach is sometimes called for, in order to maintain this distance if the coachee is becoming distressed. This means that language such as, 'Move aside from the trail, if you will', may be replaced with the non-coaching intervention, 'Now move way away from the trail' with a degree of assertiveness.

Using other tools

Tool PL2 Time Trail and Tool PA3 Letting Go.

3 Sticky Note Planning

Introduction

This tool is a flexible approach to planning a set of steps in order to achieve a target or goal. It makes use of the technology of non-drying, adhesive sticky notes to enable a plan to be worked and reworked over and over again.

Learning outcomes

- Have an experiential process for developing a plan.
- Have an adaptation of this method for combining ideas from more than one individual.

Triggers

- I need a plan.
- It would be useful to work out the steps to achieve my goal.

Underpinning rationale

Moving steps of a plan around can be more creative (and surprising) if done with movable notes.

Instructions for use

Resources

Sticky notes (say, 127mm × 76mm or bigger), sheets of flipchart paper and narrow felt-tip pens.

1   Ask the coachee to write down the steps (or actions) that need to be taken in order to achieve the target. They write each step on a separate sticky note. They can take all of the time they need.

2   Once the steps are written, the coachee can locate the flipchart where they want it and move the sticky notes on it, in a logical order.

3   Next, have a timeline drawn along the top of the paper and ask the coachee to say, indicate or write down, when they would like the target completed and what the last step is. Using a different coloured sticky note, mark the date and time on the note and place it on the timeline.

4   Ask the coachee to arrange their sticky notes for the events leading to the completion of the goal along the line. Ask them to create new sticky notes for the dates and times of each of the actions to be taken and arrange them along the timeline. Ask them to adjust the sticky notes to align with the dates and times on the flipchart.

5   Once completed, ask the coachee to run through the steps, and, at each one, ask them to anticipate anything that could prevent that step happening. If there is anything, ask them to set down a contingency step on another sticky note and add this to the flipchart.

6   Once the coachee is satisfied with the order and timing, take a digital picture of the flipchart and provide this as an electronic file to the coachee (Figure 8.11).

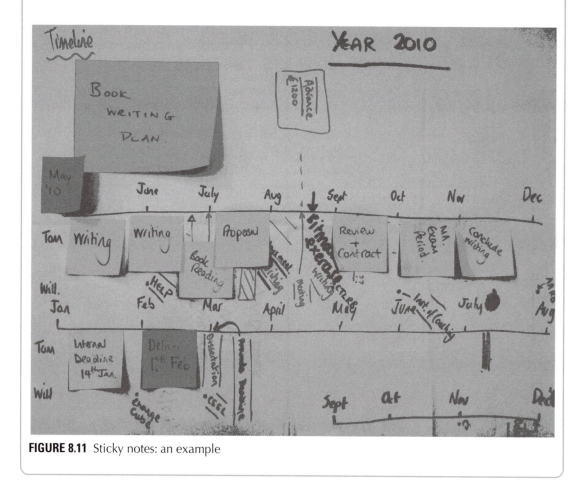

FIGURE 8.11 Sticky notes: an example

Where do we go from here?

Within the tool

If a coachee experiences any difficulties in the planning steps, you may need to go back to a previous STEPPPA stage. For example, the coachee may need to explore 'perceptions' about their ability to achieve the target. If this happens, other tools may also be helpful (see below).

Using other tools

If the coachee finds creating action steps difficult, consider using Tool PE7 Perceptual Positions – Second Position or Tool PE8 Perceptual Positions – Third Position. Also consider Tool PE1 Objective Advice.

Further reading

Best, B. and Thomas, W. (2008) *Creative Teaching and Learning Resource Book*. London: Continuum International Publishing Group.

Dilts, R. (1990) *Changing Beliefs with NLP*. Capitola, CA: Meta Publications.

Dilts, R. (1999) *Sleight of Mouth*. Capitola, CA: Meta Publications.

James, T. and Woodsmall, W. (1988) *Timeline Therapy and the Basis of Personality*. Capitola, CA: Meta Publications.

McLeod, A. (2003) *Performance Coaching: The Handbook for Managers, HR Professionals and Coaches*. Carmarthen and New York: Crown House Publishing.

CHAPTER 9

Pace and Act Focus in STEPP**PA**

We have combined these together because the Act, or Action, part of STEPPPA follows effortlessly from the coaching process. See the STEPPPA Model for more information on Act/Adapt.

PA 1 The Ranking Question

Introduction

The Ranking Question is a method enabling the coachee to calibrate their psychological state. This information is invariably helpful to the coach too. The driving force for the use of this tool must be for the coachee's benefit. The Ranking Question may measure emotional impact, commitment, certainty, or the level of exquisiteness in re-experiencing an event (or imagining a potential and forthcoming event). It is particularly helpful in relation to Tool S3 the Wheel of Work and the Wheel of Life, but many coaches use this tool very frequently in their sessions. An enhanced measure is introduced here which goes beyond the technology available up until now.

Learning outcomes

- When and how to use the Ranking Question.
- An enhanced method to calibrate the range.

Triggers

The coachee may have expressed a condition of their psychological state without meaningful calibration, for example:

- I think I am quite committed to that now.
- It makes a difference to me.
- I'm experiencing that now.

Underpinning rationale

Where the coachee explores and expresses a score for their psychological state within a range, it provides the opportunity for gap-managing any limitation between where they are at that moment, and where they might want to be.

Instructions for use

Here are some examples of its basic use:

- So, you say you are quite committed to that now. So, if zero is no commitment and ten is full commitment, what is the level of your commitment now?
- And, how perfectly have you returned to this state again, how real is it for you now from zero to ten, where ten is perfectly real?

Where do you go from here?

Within the tool

Establish where they want, or need, to be as a score then identify any gap between the scores; that is, between their earlier score and their desired score. For example, the coach can ask, 'So, if I heard you right, you have a five at the moment but can imagine that eight is achievable. If that is so, what steps can you take now to get to eight and in what timescale will that be?'

An enhancement of the tool

Our research indicates that when coachees are asked to score between zero and ten, many have actually already re-calibrated that scale internally. What that typically means is that their internal re-calibration may only go from zero to six, seven, eight or nine. Most often, the majority of such re-calibrations are eight or nine. In other words, there are many people who, internally, never give a score higher than nine, eight, seven or six. No recalibration score lower than six has been experienced by the authors. A coach who ignores this knowledge may keep pushing the coachee to go for higher numbers when they cannot do so. The coach therefore needs to consider an extra check before continuing. A typical example of how the coach may achieve that is, to ask this question: 'So, your score is seven. In an ideal, but realistic situation, how much higher could that be?'

Using other tools

Any gap provides a new target and the complexity or simplicity of these can be very variable.

2 Match and Lead

Introduction

We can help people to have more resourceful psychological states using match and lead.

Learning outcomes

Know how to encourage a coachee to have more resourceful states.

Triggers

- Erratic breathing.
- A series of unenergetic statements: about being blocked or the coachee is often negative about moving forward.

Underpinning rationale

We can help build rapport by matching behaviours to those of the coachee. As this rapport grows with them, so the chance of them following the coach (when the coach leads them towards a more resourceful state) is increased.

Instructions for use

Breathing

Where the coachee is not breathing regularly, you can think to delay your intake of breath a few times and then make a more significant and slightly more audible intake of breath. This last will most likely also be deeper, slower and calm. If the coachee does not follow your lead, repeat the pattern of breathing again a few moments later. After that, you can always provide them with feedback and invite them to notice their breathing (something you might anyway do later in a session).

Un-energetic statements

You can make your voice and tone, perhaps even your body language, more closely match those of your coachee. Then, after a while, you shift to a more energetic posture. Also, use a more lively voice to match your 'energetic' posture and see if the coachee will **emulate** you. Try once more if this doesn't work first time around. If it still has not worked, provide them with feedback on your observations and invite them to explore (psychological) state-change at will.

Where do you go from here?

Within the tool

Use Tool AT2 Resourceful States to explore new perspectives and solutions.

Using other tools

Tool AT2 Resourceful Spaces, Tools PE7 and PE8 Perceptual Positions, Time Trails (p.138) or Tool PL2 Time Trail. Also consider using Tool E4 Anchoring, if the coachee is able to alter states, at will, both quickly and significantly. The coach can also use a repeated signal, a mannerism, sound or movement, each and every time the coachee is energetic or positive. After a while, if the coachee has anchored (associated) their 'state' with the coach's 'signal', then the coach can help lift the coachee from an un-resourceful state by applying the signal.

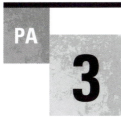

3 Letting Go

Introduction

In our rush to be great coaches we sometimes keep pushing towards actions without being fully sure that the coachee has the resources and energy outside the coaching space to be successful, in spite of their *apparent* motivation and commitment in the room. Coaching must underpin the coachee's success in order to engender more successes and greater well-being, self-worth and self-esteem. It is critical, therefore, that we ask the coachee to assess their own resource in terms of their objectives and the work/action that may be needed to achieve them. Ideally, this is facilitated in the first session and checked again in later sessions.

Learning outcomes

Understanding the importance and necessary discipline to help the coachee assess their resources before commitments to work and actions are made.

Triggers

Use at the start of the coaching relationship. Also, in the preliminary work when the coachee is introducing any substantive new objective or target.

Underpinning rationale

Coachees are more successful if they have the time, energy and other resources to commit to their coached actions. Patterned success breeds success. Repeated successes create improved confidence, self-worth and self-determination.

Instructions for use

Coach: We are starting out on this coaching process and as part of that it is helpful to establish what time and energy you have to take on the work and commitments that coaching will help you identify.

> *Coachee:* I've no time, it's part of my problem and my work–life balance is dreadful. But I have to do something, or blow up.
>
> *Coach:* Blowing up does not sound like a fruitful solution to solving your lack of time and dreadful work–life balance, does it?
>
> *Coachee:* No.
>
> *Coach:* So what is going to give, where is the time and energy going to come from?

Where do you go from here?

Within the tool

The coach must be aware when the coachee is taking on more objectives and targets. The coach must be sensitive and check that the coachee really does have enough will, time, energy and support to be successful. Offer further 'Letting Go' solutions by challenging **pre-suppositions** and beliefs. Ask questions like:

- And what happens if you are in hospital or on holiday?
- Is that really your responsibility?
- Who else could do that now?
- How else could that be done if you did not?

Using other tools

Actions may arise that will create space and energy for change. Help them gain perspective and think through their situation objectively. Use STEPPPA to achieve confident and committed action plans.

PA

4 Taking Learning Forward

Introduction

When the coachee has been coached to motivated action and success, it is useful to widen the application of their learning so they start to rehearse the possibility of using that learning in other contexts.

Learning outcomes

- Understand why motivation and success are not the end of the coaching process.
- Know how to help the coachee get value-added from their learning.

Triggers

- Wow, that has changed, and I am ready to rock and roll.
- I did what I said I would last week and the result is a resounding success.
- Fantastic, I now know to deal with <person> differently.

Underpinning rationale

Significant self-learning about how we psychologically process, make choices, motivate ourselves and are successful is sometimes restricted to the issue at hand and not applied more widely. Wider application, worked through by the coachee, prepares them for greater application of their learning and increased self-confidence and self-worth.

Instructions for use

The coachee describes a positive change in their perception and willingness to act after being blocked, or they acknowledge their new learning and success but in a way that is issue-context-specific. Ask a question like, 'So, you are ready to rock and roll now, and your mindset has changed. In what other situation might this mindset be useful?' This may be followed by a resourcing question (taking resources from an 'experience' in the future:

- So, imagine this new situation coming up, you know it is coming and you can experience that now if you want. You have this new mindset and this new situation is happening, what is going on?
- And what is this like?

Where do you go from here?

Within the tool

You may question for other contexts where their learning could be applied to extend it further. For example, 'So, if there was another type of situation in which you feel <their own words> again, what type of situation is that situation?

Using other tools

Where the coachee is lacking confidence, you might use the Time Trail (p. 138) to explore fully the factors involved in their motivation and reluctance.

Further reading

McLeod, A. (2003) *Performance Coaching: The Handbook for Managers, HR Professionals and Coaches.* Carmarthen and New York: Crown House Publishing.

CHAPTER

Advanced Tools
for Coaches

10

AT

1 **Totems and Archetypes**

Introduction

Typically, in formative years, many of us create foundling attachments to symbols that become very powerful and influential to us. Often they are useful resources to use in later life too. Use in conjunction with Tool E4 Anchoring.

Learning outcomes

How to introduce totems, archetypes and other symbolic attachments to positive states.

Triggers

The coachee is exploring positive psychological states and you may be considering an introduction to anchoring as a way of providing a positive resource for them.

Underpinning rationale

An individual's preferred totems and archetypes can be very powerful for them. They are very often superb influencers of change.

Instructions for use

Introduce the subject, perhaps like this: 'So you have experienced this positive "wow-state" several times. Maybe you would like to be able to have this "wow-state" at will, whenever you want. Some people like to identify their positive state with a totem, an animal that really appeals to them, or an archetype, like Saint George or Aladdin. Do you have something that seems right to associate with your wow-state?'

Where do you go from here?

Within the tool

Anchor the state to associate with the totem/archetype by repeatedly associating the coachee's conscious awareness of their totem/archetype with a positive experience, or 'state'. Finally check that when the coachee imagines their trigger 'totem or archetype' that they experience their anchored state automatically as a result of that.

Using other tools

Coachees sometimes buy or make a badge, card or other decorated object showing their totem/archetype so they can carry or wear it.

AT

2 Resourceful Spaces

Introduction

Sometimes, the simplest way of helping a coachee from an un-resourceful state, is to physically invite them to move.

Learning outcomes

- When to use Tool AT2 Resourceful Spaces.
- How to use it more, or less overtly.

Triggers

The coachee has been speaking at length, without solutions and without positive or effective energy. They may keep referring to one or more blocks and just one, over and over again.

Underpinning rationale

We can associate (or anchor) psychological states to any location, even within a room, or from one position to another, a few millimetres from the first. If we identify new space as resourceful and move towards that new space, it will invariably be resourceful!

Instructions for use

The coach can say something like, 'You know the expression "take a step back"? Sometimes, moving from where we are to somewhere else can help us to change how we experience things. From what you have been saying, it seems that you are in a space that I might call "stuck" or "not fully resourceful" – what would you call it?' The coach may follow with questions like these:

- Imagine then that there is another space in this room that is more resourceful, where your perception of these issues is clinical, pragmatic and effective. And when you do that, where is that space and can you tell me where it is?

- And so, in a moment, when you choose, I invite you to move to that 'success' space. And, as you move, leave behind the experience you have here, move towards taking on the success experience, that is fully in that space over there, okay?

If you wish to move someone away from an 'un-resourceful space' covertly, you can take a break and move the chairs on the way out of the room during a break in coaching. When you return, saying, 'Do you mind if we move nearer the window?' Couple this with a more energetic demeanour as you move to the new seating positions.

Where do you go from here?

Within the tool

Your coachee may have been un-resourceful in their chair and you then invited them to move, in order to facilitate a Sensory Journey or to explore Perceptual Positions. Subsequently, instead of inviting them back to the space where they had been un-resourceful, invite them to find another space in the room which they consider more resourceful for them.

Using other tools

You could invite thoughts about how this tool can be used in other situations: at work, for example, or in regard to more effective sleeping patterns. See Tool PA2 Match and Lead to enhance this tool further.

3 Provocative Coaching

Introduction

With the agreement of the coachee, a more demanding style of coaching can help break patterns of resistance. Provocative challenges are best rehearsed with colleagues before being used live.

Learning outcomes

- When to use **provocative coaching**.
- Examples of provocative interventions.

Triggers

The coachee shows patterned and unhelpful responses to the coach's interventions. Triggers, listed below, will typically have been repeated by the coachee on several occasions.

- I just don't know.
- I'm bad at this sort of thing.
- I'm too stressed to sort out my health/sport/eating.
- My mind's a blank again.

Underpinning rationale

Provocative coaching can help release unhelpful, patterned thinking and behaviours. When a coach (considerably) exaggerates what the coachee says (making extreme analogies and expressing extreme metaphors, often using humour), this can help the coachee re-calibrate their pattern and give them the potential to react positively, sometimes for the first time in their lives. The tool is supported by a genuine (authentic) mindset in the coach – one from which the 'intent' is coming from the 'heart of the coach' (see Advanced tools – Tool AT4 Mindsets for the Coach).

Patterned, negative thinking and behaviours are sometimes associated in the coachee's mind as being part of *who they are* (identity) and hence the resistance to change until this point. There must be a significant level of existing trust in the relationship between coachee and the coach. Risking rapport, from a position of established trust, can be the right thing to do and will invariably be a greater 'stretch' for the coachee, thus providing the greatest opportunity for learning, change or **catharsis**.

Instructions for use

Typically, the coach will offer specific and detailed feedback on what they are noticing and describe the 'negative' pattern to the coachee. The coach will then seek the coachee's agreement to use provocative interventions. If there is agreement, the coach will explain that the provocation is positively intended to help the coachee re-calibrate their mindset. Provocations can exaggerate more negatively but may also expose the coachee's thinking to exaggerated ridicule. Here are some provocative interventions – the italicized words are those that were used by the coachee originally:

- Is that a *miniscule amount of knowledge* or a big fat zero that you know?
- How *bad* is bad; is that totally useless bad, utterly hopeless bad or worthless bad?
- Is being *so stressed* the most effective way to get ill and die?
- So this is your *great* strategy for living?
- *Blank?* Is that as in huge white sheet of paper the size of Canada, with no trace of intelligence at all?

Where do you go from here?

Within the tool

Be attentive to the coachee's state. The interventions are supposed to both shock AND be supportive at the same time. Use silence after interventions when the coachee is processing and experiencing their reaction to the intervention.

Using other tools

As the technique is a break-through strategy, the coachee may be tired. Consider offering a break.

4 Mindsets for the Coach

Introduction

A mindset, 'head' or 'attitude' can change the behaviour of people in subtle but impactful ways. Setting up a positive and useful mindset for coaching is a valuable contribution to the coach's state for coaching.

Learning outcomes

Know how to set up a personal, individual mindset for oneself.

Triggers

Pre-preparation for coaching.

Underpinning rationale

The attitude a coach brings to the coaching dynamic significantly influences the quality and depth of any coaching process.

Instructions for use

Select some of the phrases that you find attractive (see below) and re-draw them in your own words, to make them personal. Add other beliefs, values, statements of identity and other pre-suppositions that are helpful to you. While preparing to coach, psychologically 'take these on board' *as if* they are fully true for you. Notice how your (psychological) state changes.

- I trust that the interventions I need will flow.
- I am able to listen exquisitely to the coachee.
- The coachee will go where they need to go in the session.
- I am the servant-leader.

- My objective is their objective.
- I facilitate change.
- My coaching comes firstly from my heart.
- I am prepared to be surprised by the coachee's courage and willingness to make major change.

Where do you go from here?

Within the tool

Consider anchoring the state so you can immediately experience this, at will. Also, consider using metaphoric or symbolic representations associated with this coaching-state. You might also consider walking forward, one step at a time, taking one step forward as you say each statement and pausing to notice the impact of that at each step. This may lead you to drop some statements and add others.

Using other tools

The coach often asks coachees to extend their ability to change states at will. If you have not recently anchored a desired state yourself, you may consider doing this again to exercise your skills yourself!

5 Mindsets for the Coachee

Introduction

A mindset, 'head' or 'attitude' can change the behaviour of people in subtle but impactful ways. Setting up a positive and useful mindset for being coached is a valuable contribution to the coachee's state for experiencing the coaching process.

Learning outcomes

Know how to set up a tailored mindset for one of your coachees.

Triggers

- When the coach is preparing to be coached also.
- When a coachee is coming into coaching for the first time.
- When a new coachee is struggling with the demands and challenges of being coached.

Underpinning rationale

Attitudes affect both rapport and outcomes.

Instructions for use

Select some of the phrases that you find attractive from the list and re-work them in your own words; make them personal. Add other beliefs, values, statements of identity and other presuppositions that are helpful to you. While preparing to coach, 'take on' these *as if* fully true for you. Notice how your state changes.

- I am willing to continue to learn and change.
- I am prepared to be surprised.
- I am free to be myself, to express myself and that is more than enough.

- I own my change.
- I can.

Where do you go from here?

Within the tool

Consider using Tool E4 Anchoring so the coachee can immediately reproduce that experience again, at will. Consider also using metaphoric or symbolic representations associated with this anchored state, see Tool AT1 Totems and Archetypes.

Using other tools

If the coachee has low self-esteem and/or confidence, encourage them to work at home developing lists and positive statements about their skills, character and achievements.

6 Strengths Inventory

Introduction

Our strengths are attributes in the form of skills, behaviours, beliefs, and abilities which enable us to perform well in aspects of our life. To illustrate: Frances, a computer programmer, has the ability to stick at a coding problem with a really positive mindset until she cracks it, whereas her colleague, Pip, becomes disillusioned and gives up easily. Strengths are often in the realm of subconscious competence. In other words, we are not always aware that the strengths are there until we reflect upon them. To do that, we might wish to think about what it is that makes us stand out in a given situation. Specific feedback from others can greatly improve the accuracy and impact of this learning.

Strengths are, by their very nature, within our comfort zone. In other words, we can extend our use of them provided we are fully aware of them. If we do not have that awareness, the conscious decision to do something that is a 'stretch' may not be followed through or be successful. This tool seeks to reveal the hidden strengths (as well as the more obvious ones) so that they can be used to improve, practise or lift our resourcefulness at times of real difficulty or challenge. These are inevitable, so preparedness is worthwhile.

Learning outcomes

- Know your strengths.
- Be able to refer to the strengths in times of real difficulty.
- Be confident to take on successful actions that are challenging.

Triggers

- The start of a period of coaching.
- Where a coachee shows signs of low self-esteem.
- Where a coachee lacks a positive psychological attitude.

Underpinning rationale

Being in touch with your strengths encourages a positive attitude and generates resourceful thinking. Evidence suggests (Sternberg 2003: 414) that creative thinking is more likely to occur in situations where people are feeling both positive and resourceful. Strengths can be used as a resource at times when coachees are heavily associated into negative states of mind; strengths can help shift them from that state.

Instructions for use

Encourage your coachee to consider situations in the past where they have been successful. Explain to the coachee what strengths are and give some examples. Invite them to consider four or five successful situations in various aspects of their lives. Then, get them to associate into one of those experiences by encouraging them to consider the thoughts and feelings they encountered at that time. When they are associated into that experience, ask them, 'What strengths do you have now?' Make a list of those strengths and coach to elicit more. Then, ask what positive feedback others gave them that highlighted their strengths in that situation. Useful prompts for this process can include one or more of the following:

- As you think about this successful time . . .
- What are you doing?
- How are you behaving?
- What are you thinking?
- What do you believe?
- What's important to you?
- What state of mind are you experiencing?
- How do you know when it's time to behave in this way to get these results?

You could repeat this with one or more other examples to see if the coachee can add more strengths to their Strengths Resource. Inventory, Once you have the strengths inventory set out with everything that the coachee has told you, take a copy of the inventory and invite them to use it in order that they may continue to add further strengths. Once the strengths are identified, you can ask the coachee to list their current challenges and then match the strengths to the challenges. From this, you can coach them to outcomes and one or more targets.

The strengths inventory resource

One of the advantages of acknowledging strengths is that anyone can be helped to rehearse how these can be made transferable, from one situation to another. Here is a resource drawn from Thomas (2005: 78) for that process (Table 10.1). First, list all the strengths you identify from your past successes. Second, list the current challenges that you face and then match strengths to challenges (to assist in dealing with them).

Keep adding to the list. You may like to categorize your strengths. Some people like to do that by context, for example, relationships, negotiation, selling, and strategic thinking.

TABLE 10.1 Strengths inventory

Strength	Current challenges that would benefit from me using this strength
1	
2	
3	
4	
5	
6	
7	
8	
9	
10	

Note: This table is downloadable at www.performancecoachingtoolkit.com.

Where do you go from here?

Within the tool

The tool can be used when a coachee appears to be in 'stalemate'. Invite them to look at their inventory and pick out strengths that can help them to break the stalemate. Encourage them to link the strengths in a process; first, I need to do . . ., second, . . ., then next . . ., and finally . . . Strengths are transferable from one setting (context) to another. Encourage a coachee to think about how the psychological strengths they use on the tennis court might work for them in a work context. For example, when playing tennis, they may say, 'When I am playing with my partner, I know clearly what area I am responsible for.'

The coach can help the coachee to extend the strengths inventory. When a coachee explores a strength more deeply, they may discover other, hidden, strengths that underpin that.

Using other tools

Incorporate this exercise into the STEPPPA coaching process. At any step of the process, you can encourage individuals to add to their Strengths Inventory and use that inventory to support their progress. This tool also works alongside the Authenticity Profile (Tool PE2). Elements of that process will reveal strengths as well.

Further reading

Farrelly, F. and Brandsma, J. (1974) *Provocative Therapy*. Capitola, CA: Meta Publications.

Knight, S. (2002) *NLP at Work: The Difference that Makes the Difference* (2nd edn). London: Nicholas Brealey.

McLeod, A. (2003) *Performance Coaching: The Handbook for Managers, HR Professionals and Coaches*. Carmarthen and New York: Crown House Publishing.

Thomas, W. (2005) *Coaching Solutions Resource Book*. Stafford: Network Educational Press.

PART

3

Further Resources

In this section, you will find a range of resources that can be photocopied. You may also download these from the website, www.performancecoachingtoolkit.com where a number of these resources are in colour. The resources here include supporting documents, prompts and summaries for coaches and aspiring coaches. They are offered in a format that can be used readily. In some cases, they are in a bookmark format, to be copied and cut out, and kept handy in a diary or notebook, for example.

CHAPTER 11

Further Coaching Resources

Here, we provide two separate resource lists. The first underpins 'best practice' in coaching and thus relates to what coaches do; it augments the tools in the main body of this Toolkit. The second list provides different examples of the coachee's experience during coaching, together with some suitable responses that a coach might then find helpful.

Coaching best practice: linguistic tips

LT1: How do you experience that?

We associate and recall many experiences via visual, auditory and kinaesthetic representation. Some people are naturally predisposed to using one of these representations more than the others. If the coach uses their own natural predisposition (visual, say), but the coachee's predisposition is auditory, then the process of coaching can be stalled from time to time. For example, the coach may say, 'What do you *see* as important to her?' and the auditory coachee may struggle with that. To avoid this, we need to reject language like this: 'How does that *sound* to you?'; 'What would it *look* like if?'; 'What *feeling* do you have about that?' Instead, one phrase replaces all, 'How do you experience that?' The coachee then responds from their own **representational system** of choice.

LT2: Calibration

Coaches often think that the Ranking Question, 'So, zero to ten . . .?' is for their own benefit. The question actually needs to be used for the benefit of the coachee. It can be attached to a number of words in order to help the coachee calibrate their situation. For example:

- How motivated are you?
- How committed are you?
- How real is this experience now?
- How important is this option/priority to you?
- How stressed (or other emotion) are you now?

Note: see Tool PA1 the Ranking Question for an important enhancement.

LT3: Honouring the coachee

A number of phrases support the coachee, providing them with both overt *and* subliminal messages. Some of these are presented in Table 11.1.

TABLE 11.1 Honouring the coachee: linguistic intentions

Phrase	Intent	Other intent
Where would you like to sit?	equality	coachee control
In your own time . . .	respect	coachee control
So, if I hear you correctly, you said . . .	listening	making it real
If you will . . .	respect	invitation
That is the model, where do you want to start?	choice	coachee control

Coachee triggered tips

LT4: Wordiness

When the coachee is wordy and telling endless stories, try these, sometimes repeated:

● So, in a nutshell?

● Interesting, what is the most important single thing about that?

LT5: Negative experiences

The coach can respond with these:

● If there was a positive intention in that experience, what is that positive intent?

● What can you now learn, that is useful to you from here onwards?

LT6: Limiting beliefs

Try these:

● Could you contradict that?

● So, you are the Devil's Advocate, what is another view of that?

● I suppose you could be right?

● So, up until now, that has been your experience?

● And if you did know?

LT7: But

The coachee gives reasons why something is important or describes what they could do (in principle) and then follows with the word, 'but'. The quick coach will interrupt immediately and then repeat only the positive words that the coachee has just used. This can be repeated several times. It is a linguistic tip that often becomes an embedded resource tool for the coachee!

LT8: Making it real

McLeod (2002a, 2003b) states that emotion is at the heart of our motivation and our de-motivation. If a coachee is detached and clinical about their situation, objectives or their target, the coach can try and stimulate increased emotional association with any of these. Words and phrases that are italicized are those previously used by the coachee.

- And how do you experience that *better* now?
- What do you call this psychological state when *it is difficult*?
- Can you exaggerate that <coachee phrase or mannerism>?
- Where does that *voice* seem to be coming from?
- And if that *rather hard* has a location in or around your body, where is that *rather hard*?

LT9: Making a future target real

- Where do you want to be in three, five or more years time?
- So, spin the clock forward, time is rushing along, day after day, and here is your 'certificate', what is this like for you now?

LT10: Making it logical

The coachee's emotions can make pragmatic, psychological processing difficult for them. The coach can help them to detach and become more logical. Note that the coachee may have a need to fully express their emotional state before they are ready to move away from it, to become logical.

- What is the difference between those?
- How do you rationalize that?
- What would you advise me to do if I have this same situation happening to me now?
- What would your best friend tell you to do now?
- Maybe there is a more resourceful place in this room where you could find insights into this issue. If there is, where is that place and would you like to move to that place?

LT11: Contradictions

- How do you resolve these two things in your own mind?
- What would I have to believe and experience in my mind to be able to do what you do – to have these two things at the same time?

LT12: From choices to priorities

- So, what is most important?
- What is your ultimate purpose?

LT13: Symbols, metaphors, archetypes, totems and icons

All of these representations can be very meaningful and motivating to people.

- What might that *something else* that represents it be?
- What is this experience like?
- And if that could be embodied in a single representation, what is that representation now?

STEPPPA Question Bank

There are a range of resource questions for the coach in the STEPPPA Question Bank in Appendix 2. By far the best questions emerge when coaches listen actively to their coachees. We have organized them into the STEPPPA model, to provide a convenient framework for their use.

Coaching contract

An outline is provided for a coaching contract, giving the main factors that need to be addressed when setting up a contract.

The parties are:

The Client: The company, partnership, business organization or public body that pays the invoices

The Provider: Angus McLeod Associates, which offers the coach to the client's organization

The Coach: The person engaged to facilitate learning, by a process of coaching

The Coachee: The person being facilitated to greater learning, by a process of coaching

Schedule of work

The coachee and coach meet at times to be agreed in the assignment schedule and for periods of up to two hours. Ideally the gap between sessions will be not longer than two or three weeks. Telephone sessions are available in half-hour periods by mutual agreement.

What the coach does and does not do

- The coach will facilitate in the style of 'servant-leader' without normally instructing or offering advice except where the coachee has insufficient knowledge, experience or context to understand or move forward. In these situations the coach will offer mentoring.

- The coach may use the room space and furniture to facilitate perceptual awareness in the coachee's experiences, in order to help move forward confidently with new strategies and to increase motivation.

- The coach will provide exquisite attention except when assisting the coachee to break limiting, habituated behaviours. The exquisiteness of listening may be indicated by the repeating of key words and phrases, good eye-contact and by a limited amount of acknowledgement via nodding, for example.

- The coach may be challenging, thought-provoking and persistent at times.

- The coach may sit quietly while the coachee is in quiet reflection and may not necessarily break that silence.

- The coach is not normally available outside the set times agreed, unless by further agreement.

- The coach may sometimes provide reading material and exercises for coachee-work between sessions.

What the coachee is and is not expected to do

- The coachee is expected to be timely and to bring issues or targets suitable for coaching to each session. Additionally, between sessions, the coachee is expected to make agreed progress and to report back briefly on that progress.

- Coachee targets should not be in conflict with the client's business, aims or objectives.
- The coachee is expected to be open, self-challenging and willing to accept offered challenges that may be put forward by the coach.

What the provider is expected to do

- The provider will invoice the client for all fees at the start of the coaching assignment.
- Expenses are invoiced within three weeks of the completion of each coaching session.

What the client is expected to do

- The client agrees to pay all provider's invoices within 14 days.
- The client provides a suitable space for the coaching which will be private, quiet and have at least three chairs in the room. The room should be free from obstructions and large enough for movement around the room. It should be sound-proof and should not be overlooked.

Confidentiality

The coach will keep all notes and information regarding the coaching confidential to the coach and coachee only. The coach may supply a copy of their notes to the coachee (upon request) but originals will normally be kept safely by the coach for a period of 3–4 years after which they are shredded and recycled. Any summaries provided to the client's specified contact will only result from a mutually agreed format and content, by both the coachee and coach.

    The Parties agree to observe and to be bound by these Standard Terms and Conditions,

    Print name, sign and date for and on behalf of the parties.

Conversational coaching tips

Introduction

Conversational coaching is the fluid use of coaching skills outside the setting of a formal coaching contract. The context for coaching may be formal (for example, a work-based challenge) or informal. In fact, conversational coaching is most often used or referred to by us as 'managing in a coaching style'. The whole basis of conversational coaching is that it is predicated on the belief that the coachee is typically not aware that a change in intervention strategy has taken place. In other words, the skills of coaching techniques, attention, questioning, challenge and silence are used gracefully. We know that with the skill and grace of an exceptional coach, the coachee is significantly self-reflective during coaching. This self-reflective, learning 'state' is so focused internally that the coachee very rarely notices the coaching strategy happening. In other words, the use of reflective language, repeated phrases and questions is invisible to the coachee. It means that the coach/manager must be skilled, interested and acutely aware of the coachee's psychological state.

In order to achieve this level of skill, we mostly need two key elements. The first is an appropriate mindset that honours the coachee, and the second is an instinctive ability to use a range of tools appropriately and gracefully. This second only comes from experience. We urge all coaches to experience both coaching and being coached in non-professional settings and particularly recommended is co-coaching, with a number of other coaches, to develop these skills and to secure good quality feedback.

Often, it only takes one question to start the conversational coaching period (see Seventeen Starter Questions for Conversational Coaching). Invariably, it is a gentle challenge to think differently. The period of conversational coaching then expands and develops from there.

Seventeen Starter Questions for Conversational Coaching

1 That's interesting, why do you think that?

2 Who says?

3 And is that thought useful to you at this time?

4 What could be at the root of those behaviours?

5 How else could that be interpreted?

6 What lies at the heart of this?

7 And another way of thinking about that would be?

8 And if I had that issue, where would you advise me to start?

9 How might someone remote from this situation view what is going on?

10 How are those two things connected?

11 What is the process for starting at *can't* and arriving at *can*?

12 And?

13 So?

14 What else?

15 What is the most important factor now?

16 They say? But what do you say and care about?

17 How might X interpret that?

Note: This resource is downloadable at www.performancecoachingtoolkit.com.

In conversational coaching, the rigour of checking for sustainability and the re-application of the learning into other contexts *may not* take place. This marks the most significant difference from professional coaching. The end-point in conversational coaching tends to take place when the individual is ready to move away. And conversational coaching can take place on and off when the two people meet by chance. In any case, the coach/manager may return overtly to an earlier topic later, to check if the individual has moved on in their thinking and learned more from the experience.

Exposure to conversational coaching over the longer term does help to develop people and that becomes a good starting place for raising the bar for employee development generally.

Coaching skills checklist

Introduction

The following 'best practice' checklist provides a summary of many of the core skills and actions of a coach, as identified by the authors. It is not meant to be prescriptive, but may be a useful self-evaluation exercise when analysing your practice and in co-coaching. It also forms the basis of coaching skills 'checklists' which you will find in the top ten tasks.

Coaching skills can be grouped into four parts:

1 Pre-coaching management (Table 11.2)

2 Readiness for coaching assessment (Table 11.3)

3 Coaching process skills (Table 11.4)

4 Post-coaching process (Table 11.5)

In each part, we have identified core processes, skills and attributes that are characteristic of excellent coaching. We invite you to use a self-evaluation scale when calibrating your skill level. Here it is:

A Emergent: characterized by an early awareness or limited use of the skill in your coaching
B Establishing: characterized by being mostly present in your coaching to a moderate level of competence
C Excelling: characterized by consistent, seamless and intuitive use of the process skill or attribute.

TABLE 11.2 Coaching skills checklist – pre-coaching management

Process, skill or attribute	A Emergent	B Establishing	C Excelling
I draw up contracts to include the key people Involved			
I outline my fee structure confidently			
I have a clearly established selection process for picking suitable coachees			
I have a clear and workable cancellation and payment policy			
My contracts clearly identify the responsibilities of all parties involved and the leadership structure			
My contracts are clear about outcomes and success criteria for coaching individuals and for the organization and, how these will be measured			
I set clear boundaries and expectations for the organization, the coachees and myself, and for any other stakeholders			
There is clarity in my contract about the use of testimonials, case studies and research data emanating from the work			
I have a mechanism for noting the time spent in professional coaching and training			
I have a 'supervisor' who probes my learning and my awareness of the dynamic in my coaching sessions			

Note: This table is downloadable at www.performancecoachingtoolkit.com.

TABLE 11.3 Coaching skills checklist – readiness for coaching

Process, skill or attribute	A Emergent	B Establishing	C Excelling
I ensure that coachees are handled professionally by myself, whether directly or via a third party			
I try to establish a willingness in the client and coachee			
All coachees are supported in understanding the expectations of them as coachees			
Individual discussions and agreements are settled before coaching starts			
The general success criteria for coaching are discussed and agreed with the coachee			

Note: This table is downloadable at www.performancecoachingtoolkit.com.

TABLE 11.4 Coaching skills checklist – coaching process

Process, skill or attribute	A *Emergent*	B *Establishing*	C *Excelling*
I enhance rapport by appropriate, physical matching and mirroring of body language			
I establish rapport by seeking common ground			
I am alert to the two psychological projection processes and know how to analyse the session to check for counter-transference			
I use reflective language			
I listen exquisitely, my mind is quiet			
I feed back observed patterns of thinking and behaviour			
I facilitate for the most part to follow the needs of the coachee, in the moment (see Figure 1.1 McLeod Management Model)			
I recognize when the coachee needs mentoring or support, rather than coaching and seek permission to offer suggestions or perspective, for example, 'Would it be helpful if I provided some context for that?'			
I use a range of questions to open up a coachee's thinking (see STEPPPA Question Bank, Appendix 2)			
I question appropriately, to reframe a coachee's experience, for example, 'When is the opposite of that true?' and, 'How else could you look at that?'			
I use Clean Language questions (see Appendix 1)			
I use closed questioning to check meaning, for example, 'Do you mean . . .?'			
I use silence to sit with the coachee's self-reflection and to help them stay with their learning process			
I check the authenticity of statements made by the coachee as well as the energy and physical clues that accompany those words. I gently probe where the coachee appears to be unauthentic, for example, 'I noticed that you said <coachee's words>, then your body language was like this <demonstrate>'			
I can facilitate psychological state change in the coachee, for example, by anchoring and perceptual position work			
I use different levels of challenge to expose the coachee to increased levels of 'stretch' and seek feedback from them to calibrate that level of stretch			
I handle expressions of emotion non-judgementally, non-critically and I honour the coachee			
I facilitate coachees to associate into emotional states when they need more motivation and emotional connection with an experience. I help them dissociate from emotion when it is over-whelming them and it prevents them from thinking logically			
I isolate the root cause of an issue by questioning and I support coachees to generate significant, future targets			

(*Continued overleaf*)

TABLE 11.4 Continued

Process, skill or attribute	A Emergent	B Establishing	C Excelling
I help to widen the coachee's options using questions, for example, 'And what else?' and, 'Are there other ways to achieve this outcome?'			
I reality-check with the coachee, for example, 'How realistic is this?'; 'Over what timescale could this be achieved realistically?; and, 'What would the cost to you and others be of achieving this by the New Year?'			
I use stories and metaphors to provide new perspectives if they might add context, meaning or understanding for a coachee			
I support coachees to develop Well-formed Outcomes for their targets			
I adjust my energy and vocabulary to match that of the coachee before leading them to other energies and vocabularies that might be of benefit to them			
I facilitate coachees in producing a plan for achieving their targets			
I help a coachee to explore the polarity of their experience to harness carrot and stick benefits			
I encourage mutual celebration of the coachee's successes and I facilitate the re-application of the learning from that success			
I use Sensory Journey approaches to resolve persistent emotional challenge			
I facilitate the coachee to integrate and balance organizational and personal targets			
I assist a coachee to resolve internal and person-to-person conflicts by using tools such as Conflict Resolution and Perceptual Positions			
I actively seek feedback from coachees about how I can support them more fully at regular intervals during the coaching process, for example, 'What works for you?; 'What would like more of from me?; and 'What would you like less of?'			

Note: This table is downloadable at www.performancecoachingtoolkit.com.

TABLE 11.5 Coaching skills checklist – post-coaching process

Process, skill or attribute	A Emergent	B Establishing	C Excelling
I evaluate progress against success criteria with the coachee, client and myself			
I explore other development opportunities and needs with the client organization			
I capture case studies and testimonials from the client and coachee			
I reflect upon and record my own learning from the coaching assignment, including a systematic self-evaluation			

Note: This table is downloadable at www.performancecoachingtoolkit.com.

Neutrality behaviours and exquisite listening

Introduction

Neutrality is a learned means to protect the novice coach from letting their natural, human patterns get in the way of the coachee's process. Many people find it helpful to practise this at its extreme in training, so that their natural behaviours can be re-introduced, thoughtfully, as a later stage of their development. But which natural human patterns of being can get in the way of the coachee's process?

Examples include nodding and smiling indiscriminately to show that you are listening. There are more subtle and more effective ways of proving you are listening without needing to nod or smile repeatedly.[1] When you nod or smile you are providing external 'strokes' that what the coachee perceives and believes are true and healthy. Often in coaching, these are not the case. If we have already become habituated to nodding and/or smiling with a particular coachee, one may find oneself doing this when this is detrimental to the coachee and their process. For example, a coachee who in a train of speech suddenly says,[2] 'and I tried to commit suicide last weekend and things were difficult at work on Monday but I somehow got through that' should not have a coach who is smiling at them, as if to say, 'yes, suicide is often tried at weekends – isn't it fun to survive! Let's talk about something else.'

It is also unhealthy to be nodding as the coachee blurts out a limiting belief, thereby under-pinning it, effectively showing, 'yes! That's right!' We have seen a 'coach', with an international profile, caught out in this way. There is nothing wrong with nodding and smiling intelligently (and naturally) when it is appropriate to do so. *Indiscriminate use* of these natural behaviours is inappropriate in coaching (and in other professions including psychotherapy and counselling). Professional coaches need to attend to this too.

In training, using co-coaching in sets of two or three or more (with observers) we ask coaches to try and be naturally neutral. Practice in this leads to the ability of the coach to pause for an instant, so that the nod or smile can be expressed appropriately.

Notes

1 Use reflective language, accurate summaries (including reflective language) to show you have listened.
2 This approximates the actual words of a coachee at one of our master-classes.

Sensing checklist

Introduction

Exquisite listening involves more than just hearing. It is true that some coaches manage to coach via the telephone and rely on listening very well; we do not mean 'advise' or '**mentor**', we do mean coach! To do this well, one needs to be aware of the breathing, pauses and the stresses on words and phrases being used by the coachee. Experience and intuition based upon years of learning experience help.

In the face-to-face situation, the coach has much more information available to them. Also, the coach has much more scope for error of judgement! These potential errors do not matter provided that the coach is careful with language and checks out interpretation/concern with their coachee directly:

- Oh, that shrug there <demonstrates shrug> means what?

- So, this crossing of arms <demonstrates> means what?

- And that sigh <demonstrates>, does it have a voice? What does it say?

Those who like to interpret and judge will identify one or more meanings for each of these expressions and we can almost guarantee that they will invariably be wrong! Here are ten things to help your sensing and exquisite listening.

Top ten sensing checklist

1 Let thoughts, judgements, rehearsals and analysis go.

2 Stay with the coachee.

3 Watch out for hot words and phrases.

4 Jot down in generous letters, key words, without looking at your notes, if you can.

5 Be confident that when the time comes, you will have a new and better intervention.

6 Be confident with silences where the coachee is both self-reflecting and still.

7 Be alert to respiratory changes.

8 Notice body language including subtle slumping as well as suffusion of blood in the neck, for example.

9 Practise looking into the middle-distance when the coachee is in self-reflection – how much information is available to you during those periods?

10 Memorize and rehearse some 'stuck coach' questions of your own.

Ten tasks to enhance your coaching skills and attributes

Task 1: Noticing more

A. Notice as many physiological changes (in yourself) as possible whenever you are asked a question during the next few days. An example might read like this:
   i   Head movement to one side
   ii   Lowering of voice
   iii Slight flicker of the eye-brows
   iv   Direct eye-contact for first second or two
   v   Movement of my right hand, opening and towards me

B. Repeat the exercise when you have asked a question of a coachee or someone else. Is there a difference? What?

If there is anything to learn from this, what is that learning and how can you take it forward now?

Task 2: Reflective language use

A. Reflective language can be explored with a willing co-coach. They can provide specific feedback on what they notice and you can do the same for them

B. Pay attention to your reflective language in the following ways:
  i   How you use your coachee's words.
  ii   The extent to which you paraphrase versus reflect.
  iii How you mirror gestures and facial expressions.
  iv   How your tonality, emphasis and volume reflect those of the coachee.
C. What is your experience of using reflective language? How can this be further improved?

Task 3: Using grammatical tense

Write down ten of your most common interventions with coachees and try to include some that you use when inviting them to enter into an associated state in the past or future. Check the language of each statement as if you are receiving this intervention yourself. Does the language work fluidly or not? If it grates, what changes can you make to improve it? How and when can you test that? For example you might be saying, 'As you go back to that time in the past, that specific time, when you were feeling so strong, notice how you are feeling now that you are there now.'

How could each intervention be improved (Table 11.6) so that it is more fluid and more associating for the coachee and yet, still have the necessary instructions and prompts?

TABLE 11.6 Coaching skills checklist – improving the grammatical tense of interventions

Intervention	Improvement
1	
2	
3	
4	
5	
6	
7	
8	
9	
10	

Note: This table is downloadable at www.performancecoachingtoolkit.com.

Task 4: Shifting intervention-type gracefully

Make a list of situations where you might need to move from coaching into mentoring or supporting; for example, offering experiences, stories and ideas. What language would sound authentic, as you explain that you are shifting from one process to another? How could you refine this language so that it is as clear but as unobtrusive as possible?

What does this exercise raise in your awareness?

Task 5: The Monkey Game

The Monkey Game (Thomas 2001: 12) is best carried out in training first, that is, with another coach or willing volunteer. Find an object that can be used as a symbol for responsibility. When

FIGURE 11.1 The coaching monkey

one of us, Will, is training coaches, he provides them with a toy monkey to represent the responsibility for resolving an issue or for finding a next step.

Work in pairs. Label yourselves 'A' and 'B' respectively. 'A' holds the monkey and talks about a minor issue they would like to resolve. 'B' asks open, curious questions to enable 'A' to understand more about the issue. Such questions are likely to begin with, Who . . .?; What . . .?; When . . .?; Where . . .?; How . . .?; or, Why . . .? The monkey represents both the responsibility for the issue *and* for finding a solution. Person 'B' seeks to keep the monkey with person 'A'. The monkey will move from person 'A' to person 'B' and back again. For example, when person 'B' makes a direct suggestion, or asks a leading[1] question, like, 'Have you considered x?' or, 'Would it be a good idea to do y?' If the monkey changes hands, have a laugh about it, and then work together to formulate better, open, or 'Clean' questions. Return the monkey to person 'A' and continue. After the game is complete, switch positions so that 'B' holds the monkey and talks about an issue that they have. Afterwards, discuss your experiences. Ask yourselves the following questions:

1   What was your experience as a coach?

2   What was your experience as a coachee?

3   As the coach, what internal experiences were running during the session?

4   As a coachee, what were your internal experiences?

5   Coach, what advice would you give yourself (to further enhance your coaching)? Coachee, do you agree with the coach's advice to themselves? Discuss together.

6   What will you experiment with in coaching following this activity?

Task 6: Listening and stillness

A background article for this task is provided by Thomas (2009). If you can, read the article before completing the exercise. Consider the matrix in Table 11.7. Along the top of the matrix

TABLE 11.7 Coaching skills checklist – listening skills analysis

AWARENESS:	Reflexive	Active	Intuitive
PERSON: self/coach other/coachee objective observer			

Note: This table is downloadable at www.performancecoachingtoolkit.com.

are the three listening levels and down the side of the matrix are the three positions of awareness. These are reflexive, active and intuitive. Reflexive Listening is the coach's awareness of their *own* internal thinking/feelings. This includes any internal dialogue they have about what they are listening to, and the thoughts and judgements which arise in their own self-talk. Active Listening is the process of 'hearing' what is actually being *communicated* by the coachee. Their communication includes the actual words they are choosing, the metaphors they construct and their body language. Intuitive Listening comes from the instinct of the coach and this is fuelled by experience and being wholly present with the coachee. The coach is noticing another dimension of communication from the coachee that their words, metaphors and body language do not communicate. Coaches may describe a wave-like emergence of these realizations, devoid of logical thought – in other words what they might describe as 'hunches'.

These three categories of awareness are information, but may not be coming *purely* from the coachee. In other words, the coach may miss the meanings of the coachee's communications due to their own experience and their filters on the world. Intuition then can be inspired genius or misguided nonsense and the boundary between the two is a slender one – hence our onus on coaches checking back 'interpretations' with the coachee. If you have the luxury of an observer to work with you (from being in the coaching space or working from film), so much the better. They will be able to probe your thinking about your interpretations and thinking and to challenge you.

1 Build a description for each box based upon the row and column headings.

2 Reflect upon what it means for you as a coach.

3 Consider what each may mean for your coachee.

4 Take the notions, derived from one box at a time, and attend to just that single characteristic during one coaching session. Record digitally or film if permitted by the coachee and client. Notice the finer distinctions, for example, how did you know it was active listening, what evidence was there for that at time x?

5 What kind of listening and what kind of perception of awareness were you demonstrating at a particular time? For example, when you were listening intuitively, where did that awareness come from? Maybe it was behind your right ear, or the centre of your chest, or elsewhere? Add that information to your matrix.

There are not meant to be any 'right' or 'wrong' responses to this process, it is merely meant to heighten your awareness of your coaching practice.

On the website, there is also a list of recommendations that follow the exercise. If you wish to take this further, access those. If you have recommendations, you can place those on the blog in order to offer further stimuli to other readers.

Task 7: Motivational interference

Our own motivations, beliefs and values naturally influence our thinking when we are coaching. There is an art and science to reducing the level of interference from our own experiences, judgements and bias. The motivation for that reduction is to offer our coachees a 'Clean Space' in which to explore and develop, in other words, a healthy dynamic for growth and change.

In this task we are going to ask you to try out two specific tools from Part 2 – these are Tool S2 the Values Discovery Tool and Tool S4 the Motivation Teaser. When you have completed the first of these, continue reading below and when complete, use the second tool to completion. Below, you will then find further work to develop your thinking. For each tool, we would like you to reflect upon the influences that your values and motivations have on you and your coachees.

Values Discovery Tool

If possible, get another coach to elicit your life values using the Values Discovery Tool and sheet. You can achieve this by yourself, but is often achieved better with a buddy. Once you have completed the exercise from the tool, you will have your own hierarchy. Now reflect on the outcomes from that using the following questions:

1   Does anything surprise you about your values?

2   Do these values also hold for your coaching work? If not, elicit a new list of values for your coaching work.

3   If there is a discrepancy between your life-values and those for your coaching work, how does this manifest itself? What might be the positive and negative impacts upon your coachees?

4   How do these values shape your coaching and are there ways in which they might sometimes interfere with the coachee's experience?

5   Now you think about it, what past coachee situations can you think of where your values have positively or negatively affected their experience?

6   What are your learning and actions now?

Once you have read through your responses, and after looking through the Meta-programme tool, reflect on these by doing the following:

1   Work through the table of meta-programmes (pp. 59–60).

2   Mark yourself along a line for each of the meta-programmes, for example, if you are totally 'moving away from' in character, then put a cross at that end of the line. If you are half away from, and half towards, then place a cross midway along the line. Complete this for the full set of meta-programmes.

3   Think of a coachee that you enjoy working with.[2] Repeat the exercise in 2, above to calibrate where you think *they* are on the same scales. Now think of a coachee who you have found it difficult to work with. Repeat the exercise from 2, above, to calibrate where you think they are on the same scales.

4　How does the pattern of meta-programmes match up and differ between you and your two chosen people?

5　What can you learn from this?

6　As a coach, how does this inform your practice and what will you do differently in the future?

Task 8: Totems and Archetypes for coaches

Look at the Advanced Tools section and read Totems and Archetypes (pp. 153–4).

- What archetypes do you identify with as a coach?

- If you are a leader/manager, what archetypes do you identify with?

- Are there any conflicts or relationships between these archetypes?

- Are there tensions between your role as a coach and other roles, for example, mother, father, consultant, son, daughter, mountaineer, religious observer, golfer?

- With a co-coaching partner, take one of the archetypes you identify with and use the Clean Language patterns in the tool to explore your relationship with this archetype for about 20 minutes.

- What did you discover from this exploration?

- What is the purpose of choosing a particular archetype?

- How have your views changed or been reinforced as a result of the exploration?

Task 9: Authenticity

Self-coach yourself to complete the Wheel of Work tool (pp. 52–4). Then ask yourself the following:

- What are the positives, negatives and what is just 'interesting' about the results of this exercise?

- Is there something that you should really address and add to the Wheel? If here is, what is that and how will you score your present contentment and your objective?

- Are there tensions between the results of your own wheel of work and the roles you have in supporting others?

- If such tensions exist some or all of the time, how do you deal with this within yourself? When coaching, does this conflict with your sense of authenticity?

- What are you learning from this exploration and, what actions emerge?

Task 10: Your future in Art

Refer to Tool T4 A Future in Art and draw a picture that represents you and your coaching both now and in the future (see Figure 11.2). Ideally with a buddy coach, ask them to use Clean Language questions to explore the metaphorical world of your drawing. Ask yourself (or ask your coach to ask you) the following questions:

FIGURE 11.2 Example of future coaching in art

- What does your 'future in Art' reveal about you, your aspirations and your beliefs?
- What are the implications for your coaching practice in terms of your aspirations, hopes and dreams?
- Have you found new training and development opportunities? Can you?
- What risks might you choose to take to achieve your aspirations?
- What plans might you need to put in place and what is, and when will, the first step be?
- If you apply a 'reality check' to these aspirations, what is the result?

Notes

1 A question that has elements of a solution embedded within it.
2 If you currently don't have coachees, try this same exercise with other people you know, colleagues at work, friends or family members.

Provoker Cards

Introduction

Your authors have published packs of Provoker Cards in sets of 52 per pack together with instructions. Here we give examples of some of those questions and ideas about how to use such questions in the coaching environment.

The Provoker Cards are themed in each pack. The first pack was for 'well-being' with the intention to publish about 20, themed packs. We have found these packs useful as preliminary work for the coachee, before the one-to-one sessions start. The questions begin to stretch the psychology of the coachee, encouraging them to think outside the box and to find new perceptions. We believe that this may help them to adapt to the one-to-one coaching faster. Also, some of the issues that coachees bring with them come directly from one or more of the cards; sometimes changing the emphasis from their initially expressed subject for coaching!

Here are some examples. In each case, when you answer the question, try to work around the question (to increase context) and also work down to a more fundamental level, to delve below the question to more powerful and important drivers.

- What am I here for?
- What is most important? Am I kidding myself?
- Do I want to be remembered for anything I was or did in my life? What?
- What long-term objective have I had for years? Do I do it now, or let go?
- What are the benefits of NOT taking action? What are the benefits of taking action?
- If I knew for sure I could . . .?
- Can't I . . .? Why not?
- How can my past experience help me now?
- Can I influence my health? How?
- Should I . . .?
- How much is enough?
- When will it ever be the right time to . . .?
- Who likes me and why?
- Who does not like me and why?
- Do I behave like the person I really am?
- Who would resist me for being wealthy?
- What do people think about me. Do I give a damn?
- When did I last ask someone's opinion of something I did or said?
- What are my strengths and how do I know this for sure?

Coaches are also using these in training sessions as a basis for being coached when, after many sessions, they are running out of ideas for coaching.

Coaching groups

Ten Ideas for Coaching Groups

1 Always begin with setting boundaries and agreeing behaviours.

2 Generate a contract with the organization setting out your expectations of them and defining their expectations of you.

3 Devise clear, success criteria.

4 Make clear the requirements for the room(s) to be used, equipment and support.

5 Make clear how the group are to be introduced to the coaching and what will happen if individuals are unwilling to enter into the process.

6 With the group, begin with an outline of the generic goals for the coaching.

7 Pre-frame the group experience, for example, 'Some people are nervous or apprehensive about this kind of experience, others are immediately relaxed, some are actively antagonistic or just waiting to see what happens with an open mind. I find that when people realize that this experience is about making their lives better, as well as about the company doing well, that they come on board quickly and engage with the process and the group, because it's right for them.'

8 Develop a local agreement with the group based on a principle of development and learning. For example, use the question, 'What do we need from one another today so that we can develop and learn together effectively?' Chart their responses and acknowledge what they say to help clear up any apprehensions and concerns anyone may have about the process or about the usefulness of the experience. To generate an accepted local agreement, ask the group, 'Who is responsible for making this happen?' Devise a process for responding to transgressions from that agreement.

9 Activities can increase in 'personal risk' for the delegates as they relax and engage. Adapt exercises to encourage the least outgoing of the group. Begin with individual reflections, then work in pairs before working in larger groups. If the dynamics allow, let the delegates self-select their group size.

10 Share and use a model for exploring the issues. A strengths-based beginning is often a powerful reframe. A useful model is **STRIDE**:

>   **Strengths** – What are our strengths as a team?
>   **Targets** – What are we trying to achieve?
>   **Reality** – What is preventing us from achieving the target?
>   **Ideas and options** – What have we got as a group that could help overcome the challenges we face?
>   **Decisions** – What are we going to commit to doing to change things for the better? Who will do what, and by when?
>   **Evaluate** – When and how will we evaluate our progress?

You can use the following model (Figure 11.3) to represent and explain STRIDE to teams:

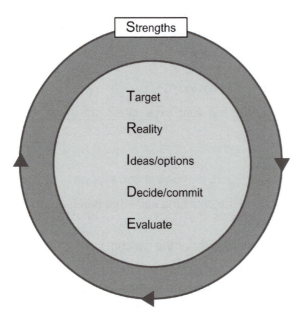

FIGURE 11.3 STRIDE model for group coaching

Note: This figure is downloadable at www.performancecoachingtoolkit.com.

- Use STRIDE as a guide, not a rigid template.

- Let the negatives and the positives be expressed, and play Devil's Advocate throughout. For example, 'So, if what you're saying is true, and if I am your Devil's Advocate, how come <example> happens like that?' or, 'When doesn't that happen?'

- Introduce the group to the concept of Internal and External Locus of Control and use these as a way to encourage responsibility in the team.

- Use a range of activities throughout the programme that gets people engaging with one another and talking about the issues, the challenges, the successes and the solutions. See your role as one of 'drawing out', challenging thinking and recording the usable ideas and agreements that emerge. Complete the session by getting the group to summarize both the learning and the actions from the session.

Further reading

Knight, S. (2002) *NLP at Work: The Difference that Makes the Difference* (2nd edn). London: Nicholas Brealey.

Lawley, J. and Tompkins, P. (2000) *Metaphors in Mind*. London: The Developing Company Press.

McLeod, A. (2003) *Performance Coaching: The Handbook for Managers, HR Professionals and Coaches*. Carmarthen and New York: Crown House Publishing.

Thomas, W. (2005) *Coaching Solutions Resource Book*. Stafford: Network Educational Press.

Thomas, W. and Smith, A. (2004) *Coaching Solutions, Practical Ways to Improve Performance in Education*, Stafford: Network Educational Press.

Whitmore, J. (2007) *Coaching for Performance*. London: Nicholas Brealey

Zeus, P. and Skiffington, S. (2002) *The Coaching at Work Toolkit*. Maidenhead: McGraw-Hill.

Review and What Next?

STRIDE, GROW and STEPPPA

We have focused in this book on the use of the STEPPPA model as a guide to structuring coaching conversations. It is not the only model available. Other frameworks exist and these include GROW and STRIDE. We would like to offer a brief overview of these two models.

By far the most commonly used and best-known coaching model for frameworking conversations is the so-called GROW model.

A popular coaching model originally developed at McKinsey, the GROW Model maps four distinct phases of a coaching conversation. These are:

1   *Goal*: providing the setting, context and short- and longer-term goals of the coachee.

2   *Reality*: this involves the exploration and probing of the existing situation in relation to the goal.

3   *Options*: this area of the model seeks to explore options for achieving the goals set above.

4   *Will/What/Whom*: this aspect of the coaching conversation is about establishing the 'Will' of motivation to take action, specifically 'What' will be done and by 'Whom'.

The GROW acronym provides the 'broad brushstrokes' of the key elements of a quality coaching conversation. The STEPPPA model which we offer in this book provides more detailed 'fine brushstrokes' for coaching.

STRIDE (Thomas 2005), which also features in the section on coaching groups in Chapter 11, is ideal for both one-to-one and group coaching work. It begins with a focus on the Strengths of the individual or team and then focuses them into a Target which is a well-formed outcome. It then invites coachees to consider the Real Situation, which explores the factors preventing them from achieving their target. It moves then to consider Ideas which are potential ways forward to achieving the target, and these are explored and expanded upon. The D of STRIDE is for Decision and this is where the Ideas are tested, with the coach encouraging the coachee to consider the implications of taking each course of action before deciding upon an action to commit to. The final letter in the acronym is for Evaluation. This has two parts, the first being a commitment scaling process (see Tool PA1 the Ranking Question, Chapter 9) to check the level of commitment to an action and the second part relates to following up and evaluating the success of the action at a later coaching session. The STRIDE model has become well known in education settings such as schools, colleges and universities.

There are similarities between GROW and STRIDE in that the middle four elements of

STRIDE broadly map onto GROW. STRIDE has the additional element of Strengths which is not meant so much as a step, but as a reminder to the coach to draw out and utilize the coachee's strengths throughout the coaching process (see Coaching Groups in Chapter 11 for an image of the STRIDE model).

How are GROW and STRIDE related to STEPPPA? If one were to map the former two onto STEPPPA they might look like this:

GROW	STRIDE	STEPPPA
Goal	Strengths	Subject
	Target	Target
		Emotion
Reality	Strengths	Emotion
	Real Situation	Perception
Options	Strengths	Perception
	Ideas	Plan
Will	Strengths	Plan
	Decisions	Pace
		Act/Amend

The Strengths element of STRIDE is found throughout, emphasizing the importance of maintaining awareness of and access to the coachee's strengths both to assist them in accessing the 'how to' strategies they might require during a coaching session and also to create resourceful states of mind for problem-solving and progress.

Neither STRIDE, GROW nor STEPPPA are intended to be used in a slavishly linear fashion. On the contrary, they are designed as broad checklists to assist the coach in serving the coachee's best interests. Such models are used more stringently by novice coaches, and become check-back tools for more experienced practitioners who find the need for greater clarity or direction at points in more intuitive coaching conversations.

Closing thoughts

As we bring this book of resources to a close, we hope that you have found it stimulating and above all, a useful adjunct in developing your coaching practice. We re-emphasize that tools (and frameworks like STEPPPA, GROW and STRIDE), however powerful, are not enough. In the hands of the average coach, they are like the bullets from a machine gun when handled by a drunk. We aver that coaching excellence is underpinned by principles and humanity. We attempted to capture some of those principles in Part 1 and hope that all of us are developing our knowledge, experience and grace to become more exquisitely human.

Interpretations of principles are, by their very nature, somewhat abstract. This can lead to varying interpretations among readers. We hope, however, that we have done our job well enough so that your understanding will serve you well and develop your advanced coaching skills to new levels. We are advocates for values-driven coaching. We believe that mastery, humanity and grace produce a state of 'being' with coachees. This state of 'being' offers inspirational opportunities for them, and they can have profound results, sometimes within minutes. This excellence in truly 'being' as a coach makes the most awesome difference to the lives of those people who are led and supported by those who inhabit the mantle. We have attempted to summarize the relationship between skills, tools, frameworks and values and principles in the metaphor of a tree (Figure 12.1). Albeit a little simplistic we hope that it helps you.

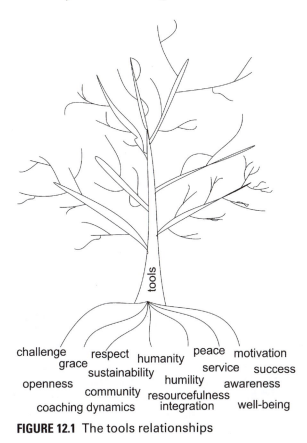

challenge   grace   respect   humanity   peace   motivation   service   success   openness   sustainability   humility   awareness   community   resourcefulness   coaching dynamics   integration   well-being

FIGURE 12.1 The tools relationships

The values and principles of coaching are the roots and trunk of a tree, then the frameworks, tools, techniques and skills are the branches and leaves which enable the gathering of light and the bearing of fruit. In this way there is a dynamic which exists between principles and tools, and this is analogous to intention and action. If principles drive intention, then tools supply the means by which the right action can be taken. Likewise, the right coachee-outcomes, selected from active choices by the coachee, emerge into the light. None of this is worthwhile without humanity; the warmth of the sunshine that bathes the leaves and the cleansing nature of water. It is the higher nature of humanity that provides the best mindfulness – and that ensures that our intentions and actions are delivered with compassion for our fellow human beings. This philosophy is core to our coaching work; we support coachees to be successful, but to have well-being too. Success is not then achieved at the cost of everything else, but in harmony with everything else.

On a practical level we suggest that you continue to develop your practice through a combination of reading, carrying out the exercises and evaluations in this book, coaching clients and also working with buddies to critique your coaching practice. Recording sessions and watching them back with kindness and with curiosity in equal measure, is a great way to notice the areas for improvement and to measure the progress you are making. Support and challenge in harmony are vital in our view to make progress as a coach. Integrating this kind of balance is also essential for your own well-being and is key to supporting your coachees in an authentic, ethical and effective manner.

Success without balance and well-being is not actually success for anyone.

(Will Thomas and Angus McLeod)

Download the resources from this book @ www.performancecoachingtoolkit.com.

Further reading

Landsberg, M. (1997) *The Tao of Coaching*. London: HarperCollins Business.

McLeod, A. (2003) *Performance Coaching: The Handbook for Managers, HR Professionals and Coaches*. Carmarthen and New York: Crown House Publishing.

Thomas, W. and Smith, A. (2004) *Coaching Solutions, Practical Ways to Improve Performance in Education*. Stafford: Network Educational Press.

Whitmore, J. (2007) *Coaching for Performance*. London: Nicholas Brealey.

Glossary

Words and phrases in bold signify a reference to another term listed in this glossary. Some words and phrases NOT used in this book are also included to provide a wider resource to our readers.

51% Rule	A mantra of McLeod (2006: 82) for assisting coachees to understand a more responsible and effective way of dealing with interpersonal issues
Acronym	The initial capitals of a phrase which themselves spell a new 'word' for the benefit of recall
Affirmation	An affirmation is a positive phrase, description or sentence that outlines how you wish to behave, think or feel
Aide-mémoire	(French) a note which acts as an aid to recall
Aligned	As in, 'psychological alignment'. To live with integrity; live in line with values and beliefs
Analogy	Similar to
Anchored	Or (noun), 'anchor'. A psychological representation that triggers a change of psychological state/mindset. These occur naturally in everybody but can be 'installed' using **NLP** techniques to provide a positive 'resource'
Anchoring	The act of creating a psychological anchor
Archetype	A (fictional) character that holds particular meaning to an individual
Association	As in, 'psychological association'. Emotional connectedness with an issue. See **dissociation** also
Attention	See **exquisite attention**
Authenticity	Being true to who we are, what we believe and what we value
Away-from motivation	Target-oriented motivation resulting from a desire to move away from 'negatively perceived' experience
Body language	Habitual, observable, physical manifestations that may link to particular psychological states in a given context
Catharsis	A leap in perception
Challenge	One of the three **Principal instruments** of coaching (McLeod 2003a: 5). Challenge is used to help shift perception (in the context of an excellent working relationship)
Clean Language	Developed by David Grove, Clean Language comprises questions that reduce the potential of the coach to dump their own limitations and perspectives onto their coachees

Client	The person or organization that contracts to pay for coaching
Coach	Facilitator of change
Coachee	The person being coached
Co-coaching	This term describes an arrangement like that of co-counselling, where two coaches coach one another on an equal footing and without payment
Comfort zone	The psychological state resulting from experiences that are familiar. See **stretch zone**
Congruence	Authenticity
Conscious perception	Awareness of a situation, its context and what is going on – often from a number of different perspectives, rather than one, see **perceptual position**
Context	The wider knowledge of a situation, the setting
Devils' Advocate	A person who asks the 'what if' question when the outcome could be surprising or difficult
Dissociation	Emotional detachment from an issue
Dynamic	The whole, and holistic interaction between coach and coachee
Emotional Intelligence	Or EI, normally represented as EQ. Emotional intelligence can be accelerated by obtaining honest and specific feedback from others. It is founded upon both awareness and management of self which, augmented by feedback, enhances the understanding and management of others
Empowering belief	A belief that enhances motivated action
Emulate	To mimic
EQ	Emotional Quotient. The equivalent to IQ (Intelligence Quotient), in emotional terms
Exquisite attention	The ability of a coach to give all their attention to listening to the coachee on a holistic basis. This psychological state is largely free from mental processing including analysis, rehearsal, self-doubt and other internal dialogue
Exquisite listening	See **exquisite attention**
Experience	(Verb) as in 'psychological experience': a holistic attention to self that may include physical, emotional and wider sensory perceptions
Facilitate	To assist people to learn and act with their own resources in a holistic way and in the broad context of their life experiences
Facilitation	The act of facilitating
Feedback	Providing written or verbal communication as a result of interaction or communication with a colleague(s), see **TIDI**
First position	Or 'First Perceptual Position', where, typically, where a coachee is recalling and attempting to re-live a situation as themselves

Flexibility	Mental agility in being open to new ideas, thinking and experiences
Follower's question	What stops you?
Future desired state	The target or goal but experienced holistically, in the present
Future pacing	An **NLP** term which is a check to make sure that a new approach or action is likely to be successful in a future scenario. This is facilitated by role-play or by the coachee's psychological agility
GROW	The coaching model developed at McKinsey and promoted subsequently by John Whitmore and others, including Myles Downey: Goal-setting, Reality-checking, Options and Will/What/When/Whom
Hierarchy of logical levels	See **Logical Levels**
Holistic	A broad view embracing the widest possible sensing, feeling, thinking about a given situation
Incongruence	Opposite of **authenticity**
Inner conflict	A situation where two or more ideas or beliefs compete
Inner Game	Gallwey's model of coaching based upon awareness, choices and trust
Internal dialogue	Psychological voices/conversations in the mind
Internal reference	Where a coachee habitually experiences internal approval before action, in a given context
Intervention	Any change made by the coach that stimulates response in the coachee. This can be physical movement, a cough, smiling, silence, question or challenge
Kinaesthetic	Of feeling, including touch, taste and smell
Leader's question	What does that do for you?
Limiting belief	A belief that inhibits motivated action
Logical levels	A motivation model of change having purpose and values at its top and environment at its base; hierarchy of logical levels
McLeod Management Model (MMM)	A description for the practical use of coaching, mentoring and support for a person/coachee and a philosophy for relying more on **facilitative** processes, when the needs are not urgent
Mentor	Typically, a colleague who will provide advice. But see **mentoring**
Mentoring	Ideally a **facilitated** process that may include ideas, information, experiences and stories which are used when the mentee has too little information or context to understand the offered developmental step or way forward from their issue. In real-life coaching, mentoring interventions are sometimes needed, see **McLeod Management Model**
Metaphor	A story that echoes something real in the conscious, often visually represented as an image or moving image

Meta-programme	**NLP** term for psychological filter. Over 90 are recorded
Mindset	An attitude – a psychological state taken from an **authentic** range of personal experiences and understandings in order to focus the mind with the best attitude (typically for a given challenge)
MMM	Acronym for the **McLeod Management Model**
Modelling	The act of establishing the **mindset** and behaviours of an achiever in a particular **context**, in order to apply it to self or others
Neural pathway	Repeated stimulation in the brain leads to fast-track recall, reaction and or emotional responses. Although a passive quality, it is possible to use neural pathways proactively to create desired, psychological, response patterns to a repeated stimulus
Neuro-linguistic programming (NLP)	A set of tools, some borrowed from other disciplines, that assist personal growth and, in the right hands, lasting change
Neutrality	Applied to the coach. A state of being that does not express, through any means, a reaction to a coachee's expressed emotion. This is in order to help the coachee stay wholly with their own material and process
Non-verbal communication	Also, 'non-verbal expression'. An expression by physical manifestation, often minor and subliminal
Open question	A question that may not be answered simply by 'yes', 'no' or a numeral
Outcome	Typically meaning 'desired' outcome, outcomes are wants and needs which may be satisfied by achieving a suitable **target** or goal. Targets do not necessarily satisfy outcomes. It is the job of the coach to check that they do
Pattern Breaker	An **NLP** device, typically physical, to try and break a habitual and unwanted chain of thinking, or psychological events, that have led to particular behaviour
Patterns	Patterns are habitual thinking and/or behaviours which are so familiar to the coachee that the coachee is barely aware of them, if at all. While patterns can help efficiency, they can also become outdated and create dysfunction in an individual. One great result of coaching is that the coachee will receive honest feedback about patterns so that changes can be made
Perception	A reality as understood by the individual
Perceptual position	A situation, typically replayed and experienced in the mind of the **coachee**. There are a number of such perceptual positions. These invariably include: **First Position** (self) in that scenario, **Third Position** (Observer) and **Second Position** (another person involved in that situation)

Power of Silence	Course developed by McLeod and Breibart which provides delegates with a powerful understanding of the value of self-reflective silence in coaching
Pre-supposition	An idea or belief that assumes something to be true
Principal instruments	Questioning, Challenge and Silence, the three fundamentals of coaching
Projection	Imagining that another person has your own emotional state and/or needs
Provocative coaching	A term coined by McLeod (2002b) for a style of intervention informed by the technology of Farrelly (Farrelly and Brandsma 1974), Provocative Therapy. It is best used where the coachee has established patterns that diminish their potential for well-being and success and only then, with the expressed permission of the coachee
Psychological construct	A set of values, beliefs and or sense of self created to form a useful and productive mindset for change
Questioning	One of the three **Principal instruments** of Coaching
Rapport	**NLP** term meaning the establishment of good relating. Rapport is necessary before coaching work can really get going but a good coach will be willing to risk excellent rapport through the use of both challenge and honest feedback
Reality	A set of **perceptions** that meet the needs of the individual for understanding their experience, and the world around them. Reality is formed from perceptions only and is not truth
Reframe	A psychological trick used by coaches to encourage a new **perception** on a particular issue, characteristic or behaviour
Reflective language	The coach's use of the coachee's language, exquisitely, to help maintain them in their issue
Representational system	**NLP** term normally represented by VAKog; the three main ways in which NLP attempts to describe how individuals psychologically represent information. These are Visual, Auditory and Kinaesthetic (including olfactory and gustatory; smell and taste)
Resourceful space	A place where it is assumed that a positive and useful **mindset** can be achieved. Moving to that place and being mindful of that belief as you do so, can create that desired, positive mindset
Resourceful state	A psychological state that is useful in order to manage a particular situation
Script	Scripts are typically referred to as useful, positive phrasing which are rehearsed in order to help in a given and upcoming situation
Second Position	Or 'Second Perceptual position', where a coachee is recalling and attempting to re-live a situation from the

	perspective of another person (in that situation) in order to gain insights
Sensory acuity	**NLP** term meaning an ability to attend to sensing in a more holistic way, not merely by hearing and looking
Sensory journey	A psychological path of reality to explore desired **outcomes** and **targets** as if real and also to re-experience previous situations, as if real again
Servant Leadership	A way of being that sees oneself as a facilitator of others rather than as a director
Silence	One of the three **Principal instruments** of coaching and the most successful for facilitating **catharsis**
SMART goal	An acronym for Specific, Measureable, Achievable, Realistic and Time-bounded
Stakeholder	A tertiary person (e.g. line manager) who has a legitimate interest in the coaching assignment
State	Pertaining to psychology: a psychological and emotional way of being
State management	Means of controlling or opening up to a particular psychological way of being
STEPPPA	**McLeod's Coaching Model**
Strengths inventory	A list of positively stated characteristics, traits and achievements created as a mechanism for developing increased self-esteem
Stretch zone	The psychological zone which a coachee is drawn into by a skilled coach. The stretch zone is often referred to as the learning zone because the potential for learning is great. Individuals are generally poor at self-coaching into this zone, which is one good reason for having a coach
STRIDE	The tool of Thomas (Thomas and Smith 2004) and an acronym of Strengths, Target, Real situation, Ideas, Decision, see text
SWISH	Or 'SWISH pattern'. An **NLP** method for changing a negative pattern of 'being' into a (visually represented and desired) new experience
SWOT analysis	A simple methodology based upon an acronym and used for the assessment of Strengths, Weaknesses, Opportunities and Threats in any given situation
Symbolic Modelling	A way of facilitating a coachee towards solutions by encouraging metaphoric development
Target	Or 'goal' or 'objective'. The target may or may not satisfy the coachee's **outcomes** and the coach is responsible for checking that it does
Third position	Or '**Third Perceptual Position**', where a coachee is recalling a situation but from the perspective of a remote, outside observer, in order to gain insights

TIDI	Feedback acronym for Thinking pattern, Impact on me/us, Desired behaviour and Impact on me/us resulting from that
Tool	A model or psychological device for encouraging change, for example, in **perception**, motivation, commitment and understanding
Totem	An animal or object of significant representative value
Towards motivation	Target-oriented motivations resulting from a desire to move towards 'positively perceived' experience
Trigger	A cue that initiates a chain of psychological (and typically behavioural) changes, usually on a habitual basis
Well-formed outcome	**NLP** term for a target for which there is a motivated path to a specified time-scale and which is obtainable, realistic and for which the consequences have been fully explored in a holistic context. The word **outcome** is used (in this expression) interchangeably with goal or target. We differentiate the word 'outcome' as being different from a target or goal in the context of coaching. See **outcome** for that differentiation.

Appendix 1: Clean language questions

This is a tool you can download to use as an aide-mémoire from www.performancecoachingtoolkit.com.

	CLEAN LANGUAGE QUESTIONS
	Questions for developing insight
1	And is there anything else about (coachee's words)?
2	And what kind of (coachee's words) is that (coachee's words)?
3	And that's (coachee's words) like what?
4	And where is (coachee's words)?
5	And whereabouts (coachee's words)?
	Questions for moving time
6	And then what happens?
7	And what happens next?
8	And what happens just before (coachee's words)?
9	And where could (coachee's words) come from?

Appendix 2: STEPPPA Question Bank

Subject

What do you want to discuss?
What specifically do you want to discuss?
How does what you want to discuss support the terms of our contract together?
Are there any ways in which what you want to discuss might have a negative impact on your organization?

Target objective

What do you want as an outcome from this session?
What do you want as a long-term or mid-term outcome?
What would you prefer?
When will you accomplish this target?

Emotional context to subject and target

How much do you want this, on a scale of one to ten where ten is totally and one, not at all?
If you are to go ahead in time now, to a time in the future when you have achieved your target, what does it feel like, or look like, or sound like, now that you have achieved this target?
On a scale of one to ten where ten is totally motivated and one is not at all motivated, how motivated are you by this target you have chosen?
What would make it even more motivating?
When do you want to have achieved it by?
What excites you about this goal?
How will you know when you have achieved this target specifically?
What will be the last thing that has to happen for you to know you have achieved this?

Perception and target re-evaluation

Establishing current reality

What is the current situation?
What do you feel about this right now?

What is missing here that you would like to have?
What are the problems this is causing?
What have you already tried to improve things, and what were the outcomes?
How does it feel at the moment?

Reframing thinking

Look back at your target. Is it still what you want/need?
What would your most trusted colleague/friend/confidant say were your greatest attributes?
Who says this is true?
What are you choosing here? What other choices are there?
If you secretly knew what the answer was, what would it be?
What are you tolerating that you should stop tolerating?
What is the impact of what you are currently doing on other people/on you?
How do you know when it's time to do this behaviour?
In what ways, now you think about it, is the opposite of this situation true?
How could you contradict what you have just said?
What's the purpose of this thinking?
So what's the positive learning here?
What's causing you to choose to do this/behave like this?
What might you need to soften or let go of so that you can move on?
How could you make this quicker and still do it right?

Promoting creativity

What strengths do you have that could help you here?
What would you do if you could move yourself a step forward now?
What could you do if you didn't have to explain it to anyone else? How would that feel?
What could you do if resources/time/people/rules/money/etc. were not blocks here? (Insert the limitation they have identified.)
What could you do if you did not have to live with the results of your actions?
Brainstorm one of the options you have come up with. What other ideas are sparked off?
What resources do you need to overcome your obstacles?

Plan

From your options, which is the quickest/easiest/cheapest/most comfortable/least comfortable/most effective thing to do?
What would be the most authentic course of action to take?
What feels right, here?
What will you do first? . . . second? . . . next? . . . then?
How will you reach the target?
Name the steps you now need to take to achieve the target.
How will the option you have chosen move you closer to your target?

What are the benefits of the process that you have designed?
What impact will it have on you/your colleagues/your role/your clients?
What are you definitely going to do?
What are the steps?
Go forward to the time when this is already achieved. Looking back, what did you do to get there?

Pace

When will you take these steps?
How realistic is this course of action you have chosen?
What might need to be adjusted?
Who else (if anyone) should be involved in this process to support its success? What will they do? How will they know this?
When will you review your progress towards your target?
Draw the timeline for this process.
How do you know this will work?

Amend or act

What has been useful learning from the session?
How might you need to tweak your plan to make it realistic?
What might need to change so that the outcome can be achieved?
What are the barriers to you taking that first step? How likely is it to stop you? What can be done to overcome it?
How sensible is your timescale?
What will you do? When will you do it?

Appendix 3: Hot words and phrases

Noticing counter-productive language

Some words and phrases used by the coachee are important signals for what could be counter-productive patterns of thinking that may block their well-being and achievement. Unless the coachee is working through an important process at the time, their use of one of these words or phrases may prompt the coach to challenge immediately (or make a note for use later).

We all choose our words deliberately. We each have thousands of choices for how we arrange our words, but each individual selects their own individual form. Many people (if not all) have particular sensitivities to particular words and phrases. The sensitivity may be because of the positive value they attach to the word and/or because they are avoiding an alternative word that jars or offends.[1] In this second case, this could be due to unpleasant experiences in their past. In both cases, the coachee may have special (emotive) associations with the language they are using – we call all these examples 'hot words' and 'hot phrases'.

Let's set out some examples straight away (Table A.1).

TABLE A.1 Hot words and phrases

Coachee word used in relation to self	A possibly inappropriate word/phrase to use in response	Possible coachee interpretation leads to thinking that the coach imagines
Achieved	Good effort	Less value
Created	Did	Less flair
Succeeded	Had that result	Less effort involved
Co-worked	Collaborated	More passive
Motivated	Spurred	More externally motivated
Developed	Came up with	Less process and less determination
Managed	Directed	Less nurturing of individual skills
Led	Championed	Less leadership
Championed	Supported	Less leadership
Partnered	Co-worked	Less dynamic leadership
Thought-led	Initiated	Less process and management
Quite bad	Quite poor	Worse
Inappropriate	Unacceptable	Worse
Suspect	Shady	Worse
Irritated	Disturbed	Psychologically impaired
Angry	Upset	Less affected by the experience than expressed
Upset	Affected	Less psychologically independent
Anxious	Scared	Fearful
Odd	Strange	More unusual than others
Weird	Unusual	More rare than experienced by others

The interpretations of the coach in column 2 are only examples and could vary enormously depending upon the individual coachee. The important thing for the coach to understand is that certain language is more likely to be 'hot' – responses are best made using precise ('Reflective') language. The words above are all value judgements or emotions concerned about 'self'. Where emotions run high, it may be necessary for the coach to let the coachee talk themselves out for a while, so they feel they have been 'heard'. The coachee may also have moved on in their thinking so the coach may ask something like, 'So, knowing all this, is your perspective changed in any way from where it was earlier?'

Another set of words that the coachee may use about self may be sensory words. For example:

Coachee: I was frankly disappointed by Jon's lack of attention to detail.
Coach: I understand that you felt disappointed.
Coachee: What have feelings to do with it?

The coach has responded with the right emotional expression (disappointed) but introduced a sensory word (feel) that is inappropriate to the individual (whose disappointment may be particularly analytical).

As well as value judgements and emotions used about self, extreme value judgments (both positive and negative) about *others* may also be 'hot'. The coach may choose to challenge the judgement and see if the coachee can recalibrate or find other interpretations that are more useful in moving forward. If the coachee is still strongly judgemental, the coach may wish to distance themselves from the judgement by responding like this, 'And when Dave is behaving like that towards you, what do you choose to experience?'

Note

1 This also underpins the importance of using 'Reflective Language' which avoids introducing the coach's language into the coaching dynamic.

Websites

We provide a set of web URLs for coaching resources including associations and training companies. As web tends to get out of date very quickly, this information is gathered together on one page of web and updated regularly, to keep it more up to date than is possible here. This resource can be found at www.performancecoachingtoolkit.com

The authors' websites are at: www.angusmcleod.com, www.willthomasblog.com and www.visionforlearning.co.uk.

Bibliography

Bateson, G. (1972) *Steps to an Ecology of Mind*. New York: Ballantine.

Best, B. and Thomas, W. (2008) *Creative Teaching and Learning Resource Book*. London: Continuum International Publishing Group.

Carlson, N.R. (1986) *Physiology of Behaviour*. Needham Heights, MA: Allyn and Bacon.

Dilts, R. (1990) *Changing Beliefs with NLP*. Capitola, CA: Meta Publications.

Downey, M. (2003) *Effective Coaching*. London: Texere.

Downey, M. (2009) private correspondence with A. McLeod.

Duval, M. (2009) private correspondence with A. McLeod.

Farrelly, F. and Brandsma, J. (1974) *Provocative Therapy*, Capitola, CA: Meta Publications.

Gallwey, T. (1999) 4th Annual ICF plenary lecture, Orlando, Florida.

Greenleaf, R.K. and Spears, L. (1998) Power of servant leadership, in L.C. Spears and M. Lawrence (eds) *Focus on Leadership: Servant-Leadership for the 21st Century*. New York: John Wiley & Sons.

Knight, S. (2002) *NLP at Work: The Difference that Makes the Difference* (2nd edn). London: Nicholas Brealey.

Landsberg, M. (1996) *The Tao of Coaching*. London: HarperCollins Business.

Law, H., Ireland, S. and Hussain, Z. (2007) *The Psychology of Coaching, Mentoring and Learning*. Chichester: John Wiley & Sons.

Lawley, J. (2009) private communication with A. McLeod.

Lawley, J. and Tompkins, P. (2000) *Metaphors in Mind*. London: The Developing Company Press.

McDermott, I. and Jago, W. (2003) *The NLP Coach*. London: Piatkus.

McLeod, A. (2002a) Emotional intelligence in coaching, *Rapport*, 58: 53.

McLeod, A. (2002b) Provocative coaching, *Rapport*, 58: 17.

McLeod, A. (2003a) *Performance Coaching: The Handbook for Managers, HR Professionals and Coaches*. Carmarthen and New York: Crown House Publishing.

McLeod, A. (2003b) Emotion and coaching, *Anchor Point*, 17(2): 35–41.

McLeod, A. (2006) *Me, Myself, My Team: How to Become an Effective Team Player Using NLP*, 2nd edn. Carmarthen & New York: Crown House Publishing.

McLeod, A. (2007) *Self-Coaching Leadership: Simple Steps from Manager to Leader*. Chichester: John Wiley & Sons.

McLeod, A. (2009a) Coaching – Be the Change, presentation, University of Gloucester.

McLeod, A. (2009b) The impact of the inner game and Sir John Whitmore on coaching, in S. Jenkins (ed.) *Annual Review of High Performance Coaching & Consulting*. Brentwood: Multi-Science Publishing Co.

Scott, S. (2002) *Fierce Conversations*. London: Piatkus Books.

Sternberg, R. J. (2003) *Handbook of Creativity*. Cambridge: Cambridge University Press.

Thomas, W. (2001) *An Introduction to Coaching*. Malvern: Vision for Learning Press.

Thomas, W. (2005) *Coaching Solutions Resource Book*. Stafford: Network Educational Press.

Thomas, W. (2009) www.willthomasblog.com/listening-perception-and-the-importance-of-stillness-for-coaches

Thomas, W. and Smith, A. (2004) *Coaching Solutions: Practical Ways to Improve Performance in Education*. Stafford: Network Educational Press.

Thomas, W. and Smith, A. (2009) *Coaching Solutions: Practical Ways to Improve Performance in Education* (2nd edn). Stafford: Continuum International Press.

Whitmore, J. (2007) *Coaching for Performance*. London: Nicholas Brealey.

Zeus, P. and Skiffington, S. (2002) *The Coaching at Work Toolkit*. Roseville, Australia: McGraw-Hill.

Index

Bold Figures indicate that the page reference is significant on the topic

Related books from Open University Press

Purchase from www.openup.co.uk or order through your local bookseller

PSYCHOLOGICAL DIMENSIONS TO EXECUTIVE COACHING

Peter Bluckert

- What are the critical success factors in effective executive coaching?
- What are the key competencies of a psychologically-informed coach?
- What are the similarities and differences between coaching and therapy?

This book provides business coaches and management consultants with the framework for a psychological approach to executive coaching. It shows how performance-related issues in the workplace often have a psychological dimension to them and provides the reader with an understanding of how to work in more depth to help people resolve their issues and unlock their potential.

It analyses what constitutes effective coaching, stressing the importance of sound coaching principles, good coaching process, the desirable competencies of the coach, the importance of the coaching relationship and the issue of 'coachability'. It also examines the impact of a stronger psychological approach to coaching, exploring the key psychological competencies required, how to develop them, and the training and supervision issues implicit in this approach.

A recurrent theme is the personal development of the coach throughout the coaching process and Peter Bluckert highlights the contribution that the Gestalt perspective offers the coach, through the use of self as instrument of change. Anecdotes, stories and case samples are used throughout the book to illustrate situations so that the reader builds a picture of what psychologically-informed coaching looks like and how to practice ethically, responsibly and competently.

Psychological Dimensions to Executive Coaching provides business and executive coaches, management consultants, human resource specialists, corporate executives/senior managers, health/social workers, occupational psychologists, teachers, psychotherapists and counsellors with the essential information they need to be successful coaches and empower their clients.

Contents
Preface – Introduction – A framework for effective coaching – What coaches deal with – Common themes and issues – The psychological dimensions of coaching – Supporting people through change – A Gestalt perspective – Index

2006   168pp
978–0–335–22061–8 (Paperback)

COACHING, MENTORING AND ORGANIZATIONAL CONSULTANCY
SUPERVISION AND DEVELOPMENT

Peter Hawkins and Nick Smith

- What are the key skills needed to be a successful coach, mentor or supervisor?
- How can personal development be effectively facilitated?
- What are the ethical guidelines for practicing as a coach, mentor or organizational consultant?

In the last ten years, there has been an enormous growth in the fields of coaching, mentoring and consultancy. These professions, like psychotherapy and counselling before them, are going through a phase of professionalization, with the establishment of formal standards, European bodies and standard requirements for supervision.

This book provides a response to these growing demands with sections that examine:

- Differences and similarities between coaching, mentoring and organizational consultancy
- Personal and professional development that leads to sustainable change
- Qualities, capabilities, skills and values necessary for effective coaching, mentoring and supervision
- Guidelines for practice

Divided into three parts the book first discusses the practice of coaching, mentoring and consultancy. A second section goes on to look at development and supervision of these roles whilst a third section addresses the wider issues of training, skills and capacities required in these roles. Throughout, information is presented in an accessible and user-friendly way which, whether they have previous knowledge of these areas or not, should enable readers to fully understand the benefits of the methods discussed.

Contents
*Acknowledgements – Preface – Golden threads of practice – **Section one: Coaching, mentoring and organizational consultancy** – Introduction to section one – Coaching – Mentoring – Team coaching – Organisational coaching and consultancy – Creating a coaching culture – **Section two: Development and supervision** – Introduction to section two – The development of coaches, mentors and consultants – Coaching, Mentoring and consultancy: why, what and how – Seven-eyed process model of supervision – Supervising in groups and peer groups – Shadow consultancy of consultant teams – **Section three: The skills and capacities for coaches, mentors, consultants and supervisors** – Introduction to section three – Developing key skills for coaches, mentors and consultants and supervisors – The key qualities or capacities – Ethical capacity – Supervision across the difference: transcultural supervision – Conclusion: Polishing the professional mirror – Appendix one: APECS ethical guidelines – Appendix two: EMCC guidelines on supervision – Appendix three: AFS code of ethics and good practice – Appendix four: International coach federation code of ethics – Appendix five: Deference threshold – Resources – Bibliography – Feedback request – Index.*

2006 368pp
ISBN-13: 978 0 335 21815 8 (ISBN-10: 0 335 21815 6) Paperback
ISBN-13: 978 0 335 21816 5 (ISBN-10: 0 335 21816 4) Hardback

FACILITATING GROUPS

Jenny Rogers

Every manager, every coach, every HR professional, every trainer, every team leader – anyone who needs to get the best out of a group needs to know how to facilitate. Facilitation bypasses coercion, teaching or chairing. It's about how to read a group, how to challenge appropriately and how to name the apparently unnameable. It's about being able to design events which perfectly match what the group needs and then to run such events with aplomb.

Facilitating Groups, now fully revised in this new edition, is written by a facilitator with 30 years of experience and cuts to the heart of the practical skills that any facilitator needs.

Contents
Introduction – What is facilitation? – The secret life of groups – Preparation and design – The room and other practicalities – Vital skills – Facilitator nightmares: what if . . .? – Wrapping it all up – Bibliography – Index

May 2010
978–0–335–24096–8